THE HOME-BASED REVOLUTION

THE HOME-BASED REVOLUTION

CREATE MULTIPLE INCOME STREAMS FROM HOME

MARTHA KREJCI

BEYOND WORDS

Portland, Oregon

BEYOND WORDS
1750 S.W. Skyline Blvd., Suite 20
Portland, OR 97221-2543
503-531-8700 / 503-531-8773 fax
www.beyondword.com

First Beyond Words hardcover edition September 2021

BEYOND WORDS PUBLISHING and colophon are registered
trademarks of Beyond Words Publishing. Beyond Words is an imprint of
Simon & Schuster, Inc.

For more information about special discounts for bulk purchases,
please contact Beyond Words Special Sales at 503-531-8700 or
specialsales@beyondword.com.

Managing editor: Lindsay S. Easterbrooks-Brown
Design: Sara E. Blum

Manufactured in the United States of America

10 9 8 7 6 5 4 3 2 1

Library of Congress Control Number: 2021939797

The corporate mission of Beyond Words Publishing, Inc.:
Inspire to Integrity

For such a time as this ...

Esther 4:14

CONTENTS

SEVEN

FOREWORD

It was a cool fall day. The late morning sun was directly overhead. The air was predictably dry, but it was warm enough that the sweat was starting to bead on our foreheads after just a few hundred yards and no gain in elevation. The only shadows seen were from the tallest of the saguaro cacti that lined the winding path as it disappeared in the distance on its way to the top of Camelback Mountain.

This was an exciting day for all of us. We hadn't met in person before, but we bonded over our mutual interest in human potential, balanced living, a desire to live life differently, and a deep desire to have a positive impact on the world.

One of the biggest advantages of working from home is that this (today, a hiking trail in Phoenix, Arizona) is our boardroom and today's dress code consisted of comfy activewear and a good pair of shoes.

There are two options when hiking Camelback Mountain, both challenging, however one distinctly more challenging than the other. Martha picked the more challenging one. Having lived in the valley for years, I knew this was the right choice. Yes, it's more challenging, but the view is better, the experience is more memorable, and it's the fastest way to the top.

By picking up this book, you, too, made the right choice. Many of you feel a tug to do more. You understand that you are designed by God for greatness and a purpose but don't know where to start. You feel pulled to explore your creative side, to accomplish great things, and to serve others with your gift. For some of you fear is holding you back. For others it's lacking confidence or a deep belief that you have what it takes. For many it's finding the time. Still others feel you need a tactical "to-do" before making the leap or taking your existing business to the next stratosphere. Good news, this book helps with all four . . . and more.

This concise read is the fast path to the top. In a noisy world of distractions, Martha serves as your trusted guide and leads you step by step up the path to home business success. She helps you avoid wrong turns, and keeps you on track, because she has been there before. Not only on her own journey to home-based business success but she has successfully guided thousands up the path as well.

You will feel your confidence grow as you turn each page. It's as if you have an unconditionally loving friend, and your biggest encourager right at your side as you boldly pursue your dream.

No one gets up a big mountain alone. It is done with a community. Welcome to this community. We are excited to see you apply what you learn in the pages to come as you do the work to use your gift to serve others. A better you makes a better world. See you at the top!

Dr. Dave Braun (@OolaSeeker) and
Dr. Troy Amdahl (@OolaGuru),
The OolaGuys, international bestselling authors
and cofounders of OolaLife.com

LADIES...IT'S TIME

If you are looking for a cool, light autumn breeze to clear out the cobwebs of your thinking, you are going to be blown away by the summer storm that is Martha Krejci.

Not content to live with mediocrity, she has created a new pathway for herself and her family. One that she is happy to share with you and her many, many followers around the globe.

Wife, mother, and entrepreneur live together in a seamless balance and vibrancy that is a shining light out of the dark confines so many women feel today.

Martha has found a new way to handle the twin responsibilities of providing materially and emotionally for those she loves most. One that is both fulfilling and rewarding. And most importantly, one that provides balance.

Her Home-Based Revolution (HBR) program is helping thousands of women all over the globe develop their independence and free themselves from having to make the most difficult choice: Work or family?

If you suspect deep down that there must be a better way, this book is for you.

If you are done with the expectations of an unsustainable work schedule, then it might just be time for a home-based revolution.

Danelle Fowler, COO,
Martha Krejci Company

CHAPTER ONE

Getting What You Really Want

was working my leadership role at my corporate job, rising through the ranks, as one is supposed to do. Then I quickly found out I was actually making less money as I rose in the ranks. Because I was in sales, when I moved into management, I automatically took a pay cut as I was no longer making commissions. I was making less money and starting to feel more anxious. I saw my paycheck every two weeks, and I knew in my position I was never going to get more than that. MAYDAY!

I think every budding entrepreneur is always asking, "How do I get more?" That's why a lot of us end up in sales. I saw this check week after week, and when I looked at it, I felt stuck. I was stuck.

Now let's add onto that the fact that I experienced panic attacks about twenty times a day. Once they started, they went through twenty-minute cycles and just kept happening. For me, I literally thought I was dying during these attacks. My left arm would go numb, my hearing would go away, my vision would black out from the outside in, and I would get a metal taste in my mouth—all of it. Once when I lived alone, I went outside my apartment and sat on the stairs so in case I died, somebody would know. The stress just kept compounding, and I was exhausted. Needless to say, it was BAD.

One day at my desk I heard a message notification on my phone. I thought it was from my husband. We couldn't have our phones out on the calling floor, so I went to the bathroom to take it, because that's what you do when you can't keep your phone on the calling floor, right? I went into the bathroom and, I kid you not, it was a video of my daughter taking her first steps. Everything stopped. It was like one of those Hollywood movies where everything went silent.

My husband and I went through a lot to have our baby, Norah. Pokes and prods and medical intervention—I mean we REALLY wanted her. Our belief in having a child was that she was here to bless us as parents, but more than that, she was here to bless the world as a whole. Our job was to make sure she's able to live from her heart; that was really important for us. I wanted her to be able to do that, but I wasn't able to model it. It was soul-crushing to not be able to show her what that looks like, because that's what I wanted for her. But if I couldn't show it to her, she wouldn't really see it and couldn't really know it was available to her. I mean, at the end of the day, kids mimic their parents, right? And I wasn't satisfied with what I was giving her to mimic.

All of my reality was right in front of my face. That was all that mattered to me. Watching that video in the bathroom felt like one of those touch-point moments everybody has at different crossroads in

4

their life, where this was the deciding factor: Are you going to stay here doing what you're doing? Or are you going to make a choice to do something different? It doesn't have to be right or wrong, but you've got a choice to make right now.

I couldn't take time off to go home and see my daughter because as a mom, you don't have sick time of your own. You're always using it to take care of your child. I had to go back to my desk and sit down. I felt like a caged animal. I kept asking myself, "Why can't I just leave?" I couldn't focus for the rest of the day.

I got home that night and said to my husband, Mike, "I can't do this. I need to be able to work from home. We need to start our own agency." I had a long history with the tech company I worked for and had soaked up the ins and outs of everything. It would be easy for me to use that and help clients on my own.

Kids mimic their parents. . . . And I wasn't satisfied with what I was giving her to mimic.

The dynamic between Mike and me is that I am the visionary with the flighty ideas, and Mike is the guy that holds the string to my balloon. He is on the ground allowing me to fly but making sure he's got me. He was the one that was usually asking, "How are we going to get insurance? How are we going to be able to make this work?"

My reality was my in-laws lived with us, and I was the only one bringing in a regular income in that entire house. We were two households—including a baby—and I was bringing in the only substantial income, which also came from the job that provided the insurance for my family. Then I said I wanted to quit my job. (This is the part where you hold your breath.)

My usually very grounded husband looked at me and said, "If you don't do this, you're doing everyone a disservice."

So let me remind you: this is my husband, who would normally be freaked out about everything, and he just said we should do this right now. That's when I knew that where I was in life was okay, but I was definitely not going to trade okay for missing my daughter growing up. The balance was off, so we started our own thing, and that is when we began.

The cost of having that stable job, that corporate pathway, and the ascension pathway most people are following in front of me was too high. The cost was missing things important to my soul, like my daughter's first steps.

Taking the Risk

In my new business, I was excited about waking up in the morning. *What* I was doing with businesses wasn't new to me but *having* a business was. I tried to figure out how you do this stuff, and it was exciting, and terrifying, and then exciting again.

The very first day I went to a coffee shop instead of work. Oh, it was glorious! I drove past my work . . . and kept driving . . . to that coffee shop. That coffee shop symbolized freedom to me. It symbolized doing what I wanted when I wanted. This was my time—what I choose to do with it matters, as well as what I choose not to do with it.

After about a week at that coffee shop, the glory faded and I needed to get my stuff together, because nobody was making money and I needed to figure this out. That was stressful, but it was so much better than the stress I had before because I had control. I had my ethics intact and knew I could bring on clients and treat them right. Knowing that made everything better. That formerly debilitating, panic-attack-causing stress was now channeled into motivating stress, and my panic attacks reduced significantly.

My depression changed to excitement around the people I was going to talk to and the stuff I was going to make happen. In the back of my mind, I kept repeating to myself, "I'm going to show my baby. I'm going to show my baby. I'm going to show her Mom works hard and does the things."

My relationship with my hubby, Mike, also improved. We worked as a team and he started learning a lot of things. He is in "God mode" with the

Adobe Creative Suite (which really just means he can create anything possible in that software); he does all of the videos among other things. We really are a team together. We even got an office together where we would hang out, and clients could come for meetings and presentations. Norah also came sometimes. It was exactly what we wanted.

It helped our relationship that I wasn't making all the money and choices. It evened things out, and we were so happy for Norah to see us share that.

Financial Freedom—My Advice to Those in a Similar Position

This freedom is absolutely here for everybody. It's 100 percent something any person on the planet can have. You just need to tap into the right stuff and be around the right people. You need to learn things from the right people, because if you're not careful, you can start down a path that looks like freedom but you end up not knowing what you're doing and spending a bunch of money.

That's not freedom. That's a different kind of slavery. You need to be mindful of the people you're spending time with and who your mentors are. Your mentors need to be people who are where you would like to be, not people who just talk about where you would like to be.

A lot of people think they want to win the lottery, and they just want to have a bunch of money. But people really just need a couple thousand more than their bills every month. That's what they're really okay with. Of course, you can build out from there, but freedom happens even when you're only $1,000 or $2,000 ahead each month. Sometimes people can do it with $500, especially when you haven't had that breathing room in a really long time. There's that deep sigh of relief whenever your bills are paid, and you have extra money beyond that coming in. Then you can start a savings account!

You don't need to be a millionaire to have financial freedom; you just need a little bit more than what you spend every month, and if you can do that from home, even better, because then you have psychological and financial freedom.

Time Freedom—the Perfect Day

I always ask people I work with: In three years from now, what does your perfect day look like? It always looks the same. They wake up and have a coffee in peace and quiet. They have their kids at home with them. Some of them have a nanny with the kids. They work for a couple of hours, then go do whatever they want that day.

If they can build one of their income streams, they'll be able to do that. Everybody desires to work for a couple of hours in the morning, then have the rest of the day to just sit and stare at the wall if that's what they choose. God bless sitting and staring at the wall! I've done it, and trust me, it's not a bad way to spend some time if you're decompressing. Freedom is working just a couple of hours a day, making the money you need and a bit more—then much more—and spending the rest of your time as you please.

In three years
from now, what does
your perfect day
look like?

Interestingly, few people say they never want to work again. Working gives us purpose, so an ideal day includes doing some work you feel passionate about that is aligned to you, then having the freedom to spend time with our families or go for a walk on the beach.

Impact

My experience is when people are able to pay their bills and they have time, they start living from their hearts. They start serving the community around them in some capacity. I believe every human is inherently good. I believe people have different circumstances and things they go through that make them who they are and give them their worldview. All of that can be shed from anyone if they're not lashing out because they're scared, because they can't pay their bills, or because they're not giving their kids the life they feel they deserve. All of those things create an insane amount of anxiety that refers into how they treat their friends, families, and even themselves.

I believe that whenever people feel that deep breath of relief from having a little extra money and extra time, they're going to serve their community. They're going to find ways to give back. It could be paying for kids' lunches or volunteering somewhere. Giving back makes humans feel good. Money isn't the best part of the whole thing—the best part is being able to give back. You don't find that out until you get there. But whenever you get there, the impact is the best part of all of this.

To have impact, you reach back into a fire that you've been through yourself, stand on the other side, and help pull the next person through.

I have a client who serves from her own background. She helps adoptees because she was adopted. She helps them process the trauma of abandonment that can manifest into different things. She goes back and helps them process that trauma, so it doesn't hinder them in their life anymore.

I have another student who helps older people get moving. She's a very physical person and strongly believes the more you move your body, the healthier you're going to be overall. She helps older people back into moving instead of sitting on the couch, watching TV, and becoming increasingly unwell.

I have another mom student of mine with a goal to pay for all the kids' lunches in the local school district. Just to pay it all off so the parents don't have to worry about it. I have one student who is helping other moms to slow down so they can enjoy their kids' lives, instead of blinking then it's gone. I have another mom who is helping parents see their kids' skill sets, then learn how to use those skills within the family. Nobody is stupid, but if you ask a bird to climb a tree, it's going to believe it's a failure, right? It's about finding their skill sets and then letting kids excel and be a valuable resource within the family.

These people are having an impact on their worlds, and just imagine how good they must feel to go to sleep each night knowing how they are helping the people around them. That's what this is all about.

Emotional Decisions

When I started this entrepreneurial journey, I wasn't thinking about how big it could get. I was just thinking of what people needed. I was thinking, *What can I teach people that they need to know?* So, I started to teach what was working well for me. I was thinking, *Okay, when I was back at this point, what did I need to know?*

My thoughts were always about how to move this woman off of this swivel chair in a cubicle. How to move her out of that and into a place that she wants to be where she can thrive. I was just always trying to give resources and figure out ways that are going to get her unlocked from that space and get her into this new more exciting space. But so far as understanding the magnitude of this business, I knew where it could go. I certainly dreamed about it. I wasn't getting too far ahead of myself. It is crazy how quickly it got to a significant size.

Initially though, I just wanted to know how I get this girl off a swivel chair and into something that feels much more heart-centered, much more congruent with what she wanted to do.

What were some of the things that got me off that chair? The answer may surprise you.

They were all emotional. I didn't think that going into business for myself was going to be an emotional decision. I didn't think I was going to be able to say I'm done with this old way of working, and then start taking action.

I thought that I was going to have to wait for this to line up with this, to line up with that, to line up with the other thing, and to have this perfect symphony of circumstances for me to make the big decision. If all of that came together perfectly, then I could do what I wanted to do.

What I realized was that I didn't need to wait for circumstances to line up. The big breakthrough came from an emotional space—it came from seeing the video of my daughter taking her first steps and saying, I'm done. I'm finished with this, and I don't want to miss another moment of my daughter's life by being stuck in a job I'm not passionate about.

Then just moving from there and saying, I'm doing this. Your position is so much stronger when you move from an emotional space rather than a logical space.

The average person who wants to run a business, who wants to start their own home-based revolution, is often waiting for the perfect alignment of events: enough money in the bank, a guaranteed audience, accessing and understanding all the tools . . . everything. But what I'm saying is the biggest decision you'll have to make is in your mind and in your heart. Your mindset is an emotion-based decision about what you're going to do. And then why you're going to do it.

Once you've made that decision there will be other mindset hurdles that you'll need to overcome.

Yeah, I used to think mindset was so dumb. In my logical brain, I was like, *But how can an emotional decision effect a business outcome?* For example, there's a thing called fear of success. And people will talk about fear of success like it's a legitimate thing. My initial response was *Who on earth would be scared of succeeding? Isn't that kind of like what we want?* It wasn't really real to me until I started to understand how powerfully your mindset impacts every area of your life.

What I discovered was that the fear of success doesn't come from your conscious mind. It's your subconscious mind that's scared of success. It's your ego, saying, *I don't want to be eaten by a bear. I don't want to put you in danger.* And while success looks pretty cool from the outside, there is actually a bit of danger involved, as far as your subconscious mind is concerned. Because if I were to step out, if I stick my head up, if I step away from the crowd, if I go do something different, then I don't know what that world is like. And even if I succeed there, what does that mean? Whatever it is it will be different, and different is a place of fear.

It could mean that the messages you've had from your childhood are causing that fear. It could be deeply rooted in what your parents thought about wealthy people— that you don't want your parents to not like you because they didn't like the rich person down the street. And if you become rich because of this impending success, you will be ostracized by your own family. I know it sounds crazy, but it's the mind, and that's how it works. All I'm saying is understand it for what it is so that it no longer has a negative hold on you.

What was initially really important to me was understanding and really learning what my values are. To understand how I choose to be in this world, and that's all mindset.

When I first started working in mindset, I thought this stuff is a little weird. It feels too easy. Does this actually work? It's soft skills, right? So the question I kept asking myself was: Is this really going to do something? Then I learned about the actual science of neuroplasticity. And once I learned about the science of neuroplasticity, there was no turning back. I understand that we choose our world based on our words; you speak life over your world, or you speak death over it. Our highly developed language skills have helped us evolve as a species, but the way we talk to ourselves—and the way we use language—has a real impact on what we do.

Some simple things anyone can do to have an impact on their future are to use some techniques such as affirmations.

The Power of Affirmations

Affirmations are a simple technique that has a powerful effect. Create a series of phrases that both support what your strengths are and help you visualize who you need to become in order to achieve your goals. A pro tip: don't use somebody else's affirmations. Make sure that they're your own. Using somebody else's words over and over again will not help your mindset one bit, because your subconscious won't believe it. What you do is you decide what you want your life to be like, you decide how you're going to serve, you decide how you're going to show up in the world. For example, I choose to apply an ethical background to everything I do, so I choose to show up in a way that's ethically in alignment with my soul. A deep desire for me is to always give back. I'm a spiritual person, so I always have that aspect as well.

But you can do whatever you want. The technique helps you see your future life. You choose what your life is going to be in one year, three years, five years—really the time doesn't matter. It's whatever your brain can accept. It's whatever your brain can handle. And then you mentally rehearse what it will be like. You create affirmations that help you visualize your new future.

If you are feeling resistance, then extend the timeline. If your future is a full 180 degrees from where you are today, that's pretty drastic. You may need to extend the timeline a little further down the road—it may need to be five years out in order for your brain to be like, *Okay, I can see that now!* Whatever it is, the time frame makes no difference; we're just getting our brain to accept it.

You choose what your life is going to be like at that point, and then you just start choosing affirmations: "I show up in my world like this," or "I am wise," "I am wealthy," "I am resilient," "I am relentless," "I am always seeking the best in other people." These *I am* statements are puzzles that your brain will start to find ways to solve for you. Affirmations are also a direct conversation with God—claiming the gifts you've been given and declaring you are using them.

Whenever you start using affirmations, here's a hack that will help initially. Your conscious brain is going to be like, *Oh my gosh, no. You're not wise or wealthy.* That's a very common experience. But what you do is you just keep bearing down, bear down and get through it, keep doing it. Sometimes it is you versus your own mind. And it's winner takes all. Your choice is to win this battle, so you'll eventually win the war. This is essentially creating a habit and muscle memory for this activity that will then change your whole world.

There's been a lot of work done in the sporting industry about mental rehearsal (think affirmations). One study actually compared physical rehearsal versus mental rehearsal. They got a group of basketball players to mentally rehearse shooting. And then they got another group to physically practice shooting baskets. They found that the group who did the mental rehearsal were 23 percent more accurate over five weeks of the study. So the scientists are saying, "Okay, this is good for sports people." How about this being good for regular people? If we use mental rehearsal in our daily lives, then you can expect similar results. And affirmations are an easily accessible tool anyone can use.

I am statements are really built on this idea of mental rehearsal and the power of that. The more you position these ideas in your mind, the more your brain will start to make those things congruent. Your brain will find ways to make those statements true. If you are one of the many people who have thought *Oh, isn't this a little nutty? Isn't this a little crazy?*, the fact is, we now have very rigorous science which supports that it's actually an extremely powerful way to alter your mindset.

Skills to Dream Big

Moving from where you are today will obviously take a big mind shift. But it will also take some business skills, some marketing skills, and some development of a range of new skills.

What I see in people is that every single one of them has immense value and immense marketability, but they don't know it.

A lot of people will come into one of my programs and not see that value in themselves. They come hoping that they can find something for themselves, and what we do is we uncover their deepest passion; we uncover their deepest desire to serve the community. And then we show them how to be able to create income streams around that.

Whenever we see what it is, or we uncover what it is, it's always like, tearfest. We know we've got it right when I hear things like "I've always wanted to do that, but I never understood how," or "I've always wanted to do that, but I didn't think I could do it as an income stream or as a business," or "I didn't think I could make money doing it."

People's biggest dreams are the things that they cover up the most. And then whenever we uncover what it is, they say, "I've always wanted to do that." I think it's almost like trauma—like there's just so much scar tissue over it; there's so much hurt around it. Maybe people have been told "You can't do this," or "Who do you think you are?" or "What do you know?" Maybe people say these things to themselves. But either way, there's so much scar tissue over it that they don't even recognize it. And then we uncover it. And they're like, "Oh my gosh, I've always wanted to do this." Okay— good! Go do that!

Billy McLean
SMART GIRL TURNED MUM ENTREPRENEUR

I was a smart girl. I had a good degree. I received a scholarship to go to university and got a job as an engineer. One of my dreams was to go overseas and help develop solar power engineering in developing countries. But being a woman in the industry was challenging, especially after I had children.

There was so much to relearn after taking even a short leave—it was almost like starting from the beginning again. It didn't sound like fun anymore. Even if I were to achieve success, it would involve long hours, time away from my children, and it wouldn't be my success. I needed something different, not the career pathway that smart girls were supposed to take.

I started looking at network marketing but quickly realized I wanted to help people my way, not someone else's way. It would mean I'd have

Photo courtesy of Belinda McLean

to take the entrepreneurial leap into my own business.

Success used to look like a good degree and a good job. But what I found was that didn't allow for me to be a mum, it didn't allow me to chase my dreams, it didn't allow for the flexibility of time to develop a family and to chase down some of my own creative pursuits. In fact, the old version of success felt a little bit like a trap, like I was in a box that I couldn't get out of.

I'm married with two children. I am a business and life coach. My coaching business helps other like-minded women take their ideas and helps them set up their own businesses.

I now run a global business from home that has given me enormous flexibility when it comes to time. I'm starting to generate money; I even wrote a book this year. I think everyone who lived through 2020 would agree that it was a really interesting year. We had a pretty harsh lockdown in Melbourne, Australia, and we weren't able to go outside our homes. It seemed very appropriate to join Home-Based Revolution at the time.

It gave me the chance to be excited about being productive when we weren't able to go anywhere. I was able to network with women all over the world who were in similar situations of wanting to move forward but not being sure how to proceed. One of the first projects that I've done is to write a book about how to turn your ideas into businesses that generate income and not be stuck in the 9 to 5.

My new clients are in South Africa, the US, Canada, and Australia. I look at the world differently since starting HBR. Being able to connect with other like-minded women and collaborating with them has made all the difference.

Success for me is being able to be myself in the space that I'm in, rather than what a corporation needs me to be. For me personally, it's being home when my kids come home from school and being able to be there in the morning to help them get ready for the day. I couldn't be a stay-at-home mum and do nothing else. I know some people can—it's just not me. I need to have an outlet for my brain and the flexibility to work from wherever I am, whether that's home or on holidays.

Having the flexibility to help people my way has been the best part. I can build a global business around a particular skill set that is highly marketable and desirable but doing it differently than how it was taught at school.

My husband and I agreed we wanted to not only survive but to thrive. Having kids changed things. Having two incomes is nice but once you have kids, you realize that you don't see each other much, and when you do, you're exhausted. Instead of being able to use the weekends for family time, you're busy preparing for the next week. Traditional jobs only give you so much leave time to go on holiday or have fun. We didn't want to do that forever. The ability to spend time with our children while they're out of school was key. This mindset was the opposite to how we were brought up. It was always: get a safe, secure job that provides you the money to go on holiday those four weeks a year.

What happened in 2020 has shown us that traditional jobs may not be as secure as we previously thought. It's taught us to not have all your eggs in one basket. Not to rely on one income source, or job, for all our needs.

With multiple income streams, you have more security than having all your eggs in one basket. Ultimately, it's not about the money; it's about what you can do with the money you have. The more money I have, the more generous I can be with it. Money is just a tool, like time and energy. It's about freedom and having a choice how I spend my time.

Having multiple streams of income is like a prism: you shine the white light in one side and out the other comes a rainbow of colors. Applying your skills can be developed into multiple streams of income. For example, I'm an ideas coach. Coaching itself can be for groups or individuals. My book is one income stream. I have online courses that people can purchase to learn about different parts of their business, like how to spruce up their website or create a podcast. I also do pop-up workshops and speaking engagements. One idea can be the central component of multiple streams of income. It's completely different than anything we were taught about entrepreneurship.

I realized recently that an entrepreneur is actually someone who is just serving other people in a way that is wholeheartedly themselves. You define what success means to you, then acquire the tools to achieve it.

When people say you can have your career and your family life and everything else all working at 100 percent, that's not really true. At least it's not for me. You need to have boundaries between family life and work life. On the flip side, some people think you can't have both a family and a career and do great at both, but that hasn't turned out to be true either.

What I want readers of this book to know is this: You have so much more potential than you know. Starting the journey is important, but you also need to take the next step. You can't climb a mountain by jumping to the top. You take it one step at a time. Some of those steps will be hard. You may look around and see other people around you climbing the mountain, but they have their own path. If you leave your path and try and go down theirs, the world won't see what you have to offer.

CHAPTER TWO

Nothing Changes
If Nothing Changes

Fears and Frustration

For most of my clients, their biggest fear is that they peaked when they were younger, and it is only downhill from there. The world is not made for them, and they are afterthoughts. They fear not being seen for who they are and what they would like to bring to the world.

I had a conversation with a twenty-two-year-old who felt she had peaked in college. For her it was always about having to do the next thing, but at a certain point there may not be a next thing. When she was in college, she kept hearing from her mom, "What are you going to do next?" Now she was three years into her career, and she didn't have anything to do next.

While she was hearing this specifically from her mom, it is also a societal pressure. That is why we stay busy. But we stay busy with things that don't actually move the needle. We stay busy and time passes, then it is ten years later, and you feel like you haven't done anything. That is the life the media/society plans for us. It is what they project on us, so it takes strength of character to say, "Okay, I'm actually going to do something different. I am not succumbing to everybody else's perceived belief. I'm doing this doggonit!"

Another fear is you will look stupid if you stick your head out and try to do something, you make yourself a target for others' unkind words. Some people know this as tall poppy syndrome. Think of it this way: Have you ever seen a bucket of crabs? If there is one crab in a bucket, it's fine, calm and peaceful. If you put more crabs in the bucket what you'll notice is that they start to climb over one another to try to get out. It becomes an unholy mess. One tries to crawl out, and immediately the other crabs will reach out to pull it back down. Every time one tries to climb higher to escape the mass, the others grab it and pull back. We see this in the nature of some people in the world. They see you stick your head out and say, "I'm going to do this thing," and their immediate response is to pull you back down. They may find all the reasons why this thing won't work or list out all the ways you'll fail. People can be just like the crabs in the bucket. It's safer for them when they pull you back down with the crowd. It can be scary to watch other people rise. What these people don't realize is that the image of crabs in a bucket is a reflection of their own life. They get upset not because someone else is on the rise, but because they, by contrast, are not.

The Loud 5 Percent Audience

Social status—or the possibility of looking like an idiot in front of people—is the biggest driver in keeping people small and not living into their massive potential.

Three percent of your audience love you to death. They want to do everything with you, and if you're doing something, they want in. They are your biggest cheerleaders. Go ahead, think of yours now: Who are your 3 percent?

The 5 percent on the other side wish you would just shut up already. Even if you could make them look twenty years old for the rest of their lives, they would still be mad about it. This 5 percent represents your haters. You are triggering them, and they are just mad. We all know these people, yes?

The remaining 92 percent is the rest of your audience. They just need to hear more information. Now let that marinate: 92 percent. Just. Need. More. Information.

A lot of us get paralyzed by the 5 percent because they are so loud, and we are so unsure of ourselves. But when we do this, we do a disservice to that 92 percent who just needed to hear more information. We let the 5 percent freak us out, and the other 92 percent don't get to change because of what we have to offer.

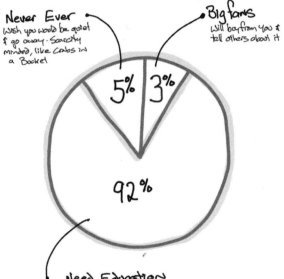

Never Ever
Wish you would be quiet & go away. Scarcity minded, like crabs in a bucket

Big fans
Will buy from you & tell others about it

5%   3%

92%

Need Education
The Vast Majority of People Need More information from you before they will take action

The 92 percent are much quieter; they may be almost invisible. They creep along and you may not know they are there until they are ready to connect. But you are letting that noisy 5 percent stop you from acknowledging the 92 percent. Look at the numbers and realize your haters are only a small portion of your audience. Like silly small—*5 percent!* You've got to put it in perspective if you're going to be successful at anything at all.

You might look at someone you admire and think they don't have a 5 percent. Everybody has a 5 percent. You have to understand it is part of the game. It can't be 100 percent unicorns and rainbows. Five percent are going to hate what you do. What I do is mentally put their opinions in a shoebox, and I shove it under the bed, because that is where those opinions belong. There is this trick on Facebook where you can hide their comments and they don't even know no one can see their comments. They look at their comments and wonder why no one is siding with them. Little do they know that no one can see them. Just a little fun thing to do when they get loud on a post.

Another thing I do is I imagine them as a four-year-old version of themselves before they took on all of the negativity. They are just reflecting to me the experiences they had. So if I can just look at them, love them like the four-year-old toddler they were, I realize it's not even about me. It is easier for me to push it aside rather than simmering over it. We don't expect toddlers to be reasonable and have it all sorted out; it doesn't mean we love them any less. When they have a tantrum at the store, we are patient with them, and bring them home at the end of it, right?

In the book *The Four Agreements* by Don Miguel Ruiz, one of his agreements is, "Don't take anything personally." He says nothing anyone does is because of you. You might be the target of their frustrations, but it has nothing to do with you. Once you realize this, you can look at them with compassion, like the toddler having a tantrum in the store. One day they will grow out of it. But for now, just don't let them paralyze you, because you have a purpose for being here and big things are coming for you!

Motivation for Change

The main motivator for my clients seems to be proving to themselves and others that they can do this. This is a far more powerful motivator than money. The dollars are only important because of what they represent and what they can do right now to pay the bills every month.

Women want to bring their husbands home from work so they can be together as a family unit. We didn't start out as human beings working in corporate gigs forty hours a week. We started out in tribes and close-knit communities, raising our kids, being around each other, and learning from each other. Many women don't realize this, but essentially, they are just trying to put the band back together, so to speak.

I even have husbands in the program that are starting their own thing alongside their wife or helping their wife. They're starting to see their wife knows what they're doing, but they're actually able to get creative and start experiencing freedom themselves at the same time.

43

My hope for you reading the book is you'll see me modeling what it looks like to live a life of impact and freedom. I hope you will see it doesn't have to take up all of your time, and you can still bring in a great amount of money, so you don't have to worry about anything.

We've done things like paid for people's surgeries, and we've paid people's mortgages off. There are all sorts of things you can do whenever you have extra cash. There are ways you're able to bless the people around you. We didn't know the person whose surgery we paid for, but she was on her deathbed and she didn't have the money for it, and we did, so we took care of her. Money in the hands of good people can do amazing things.

You can live that way and not have to work your fingers to the bone. You can feel good in what you're doing every day. That is what it comes down to. You don't have to feel depressed and anxious about your life. You can feel good every day, be in service, and live your purpose—whatever that looks like for you. You're also able to find your purpose in the first place or remember what that dream was.

Sharing Your Genius
with the World

I think uncovering these zones of genius that everybody has, this wisdom and life experiences that they can share, is the first step. For most people, the next question is "But how do I get that message out there?" In terms of dreaming big dreams? That marketing piece is really one of the big skills gaps that people need to learn and refine.

Marketing is much simpler than people would have you believe. Marketing is simply communication and actually speaking to one person.

A lot of people will say marketing is billboards, TV ads, magazines, and social media platforms. Those are vehicles; those are channels of marketing. Marketing is speaking to an individual. It's as simple as that. It's just speaking to a person and making sure that whenever you're speaking to them, you are keeping very clear in your mind WIIFM—What's In It For Them.

What do they come away with? We're not talking about what we did: I created this thing, I spent this much time on it, etc. That's what people are tempted to say, because they want the pat on the back—Oh, you're so great—but that's not marketing. Marketing is speaking to somebody and saying, "This is going to help you; this could be what you're looking for." That's the heart and soul of marketing.

When you're writing an email, when you're writing a blog post, when you're doing a video—you want to have one person in mind; you want to be speaking to one single person that you help.

And the second thing that I think is so important is to communicate in the audience's language, not yours. To communicate from the "what's in it for me" perspective is a very powerful perspective.

People's brains are on high alert for *But what does this mean for me?* And if you speak in a language that doesn't connect with them, if you are talking like an expert, not like a beginner, then your message is going to go over them. I guess it would be like a professional surfer trying to teach professional skills to a seven-year-old—it's just too deep. It's too much. Your job in marketing is to translate what you're doing into simple language, easily implementable ideas that really connect with your audience.

When dreams become reality, the possibilities really open up, like taking a group of people to Israel, like working in reality TV, like having a book deal. That's right: all of these things are happening because of me living my life the Home-Based Revolution (HBR) way.

All that I ever wanted was to help people—that's all. It's all that I ever, ever, ever wanted. There was a time where I was learning to drive. My mom and I were driving in the parking lot at the mall at Christmastime. So you know, it gets busy. And there were lots of cars trying to get in and out and all that stuff. We were in this circle that goes around the mall in order to get to a street and then get out. We got to this stop sign, and I let somebody go ahead of me. And then I let somebody else go ahead of me. And then I let somebody else and somebody else. My mom said, "What are you doing?" I just want people to feel good. I just want to be something in someone's life where they feel like, *Ah, humanity is okay.* It's all I've ever wanted. And so now I can do it at scale.

I've recently been asked to be involved in a reality TV show, and that is totally surreal to me. The book deal is also surreal to me, even though I'm living this it's still like all of this stuff is surreal. But what isn't surreal to me is the fact that I get messages from people saying "I just brought my husband home from work, and he doesn't have to work anymore." Or "my husband who has never had any sort of belief in his own gifts, like piano skills, is now out there doing his piano stuff based on HBR. And he gets to share his artistic side." Families are creating better relationships. That's what matters to me more than anything else. The rest of this stuff is cool and awesome and crazy, but what matters most is the positive impact on humanity.

Everything that's happening to me will sooner or later likely be happening to others in the HBR program. The story here is that by tapping into what you're particularly good at, what you're uniquely built for, and by actually embracing this generosity, and developing a serving mentality, extraordinary things can happen in your world. That's what we want for you reading this book—to just get a glimpse of what's possible. Because back when I was sitting on that chair in the office working for a big corporation, I didn't quite believe this was possible.

Never. And never in a million years did I imagine the list of possibilities that are in front of me now.

Tobi Feldman
FROM FRACTURED FAMILY TO RECONNECTION

My brand is Resilient AF Midlife Mamas and it's all about supporting middle-aged women that are raising teens or young adults who are struggling with executive functioning for various reasons, whether it's neurodiversity or mental reasons, like anxiety, depression, brain injury, or if it's just a stressed out, not fully cooked teenage brain. As a mother to teenagers, I know exactly what executive functioning looks like. It can show up in mild ways, like being stressed about school, or it can turn into full-blown mental illness that needs management and care.

Photo courtesy of Tobi Feldman

My career was in speech language pathology, but I put it on pause to raise and homeschool my kids. Even as a professional, I couldn't see the full extent of the issues with my middle child. With him, we had an extreme case of what they call twice exceptional. He had major executive functioning issues, like school refusal. We talked a lot about mental health over academics for years, and ultimately, he dropped out. It was twelve years of my life that were pure chaos and crisis. For me, my bat signal (an HBR term for who I serve) was about becoming the person I was always looking for when I was seeking support about my son.

My middle child has very high needs. There's a whole range of things that come with that. It requires a lot of research and support and I was discovering that the support aspect wasn't as easy to find. That's where HBR comes into play.

I started doing private practice when my children were a bit older, which meant clients one at a time. It was hard to maintain consistency and flexibility. Speech pathology is very one-on-one. You have to give it an enormous amount of focus and energy when helping a child develop the right physiological and neurological speech patterns. It's very emotionally and physically draining. You can only take on so many clients in any given week. It was taking physical and mental energy away from what was going on at home.

My husband and I both have autoimmune issues that get triggered by stress. It got to the point where I realized it just wasn't working. I had a network marketing business on the side, but I wouldn't call it successful for me.

We were overworked. At one point my husband was diagnosed with a rare autoimmune disease that rendered him speechless for five to six months. He couldn't work because he couldn't talk. He was on disability for a while. It was really scary because we didn't have anything to fall back on. We were going into medical debt with both of our autoimmune issues. It has been a crazy decade. I had a family that needs me to give everything I've got, a husband who was not well, and work that was too demanding.

I started doing Aroma Freedom Technique (AFT) sessions (in HBR) to really work on my mindset. I had heard about mindset before but thought it was a bit fluffy. I was doing meditations and using my oils, but there was something next level that happened in those sessions. I'd do them maybe once a month. At the time, my middle child was in foster care and I had no communication with him at all; he wanted nothing to do with us. During my meditation sessions I kept having breakthroughs centered on my child and my family. So in May, for my birthday, I treated myself to a one-on-one focus session with one of the best mind coaches in the business. I had a massive breakthrough.

She does something called imagination activation and it was all about envisioning my child joining a party we were having, but I couldn't even envision him approaching the table. But I trusted her and kept doing it.

A few weeks later he reached out to my husband and they started connecting. Right before his eighteenth birthday, he reached out to me and we got together, and now he's back in my life. He sends me texts and calls to say he loves me, and I honestly don't think we would have come to this place if I hadn't been doing the mindset work.

These sessions really unlocked a lot of trauma that I was holding on to. As I was releasing the trauma, I was also embracing the possibility of connection by sending spiritual messages to my son. These visualizations have proven to be so transformative. By just knowing that he was getting the message that I loved him no matter what and that he was welcome back into my life, I was able to allow myself to let go of the fear and trauma and visualize him coming back. I can just be present with him now and not live in the past.

That's the real issue for any parent dealing with a child facing similar challenges: you don't know what the next phone call or knock at the door will bring. Letting go is such a small phrase but also a monumental concept. We get so caught up thinking about the ways that past traumas have affected us that we don't try and release it and move forward through the cobwebs.

For me, it took radical self-care. I love the analogy of when you're sitting in an airplane and the flight attendant says you should secure your mask first before helping a child with theirs. Even though your first instinct may be to not look after yourself first, the reality is, if you don't get your oxygen on first, you can't help anyone. That was the discovery that was so profound.

What's more, if we're doing the radical self-care, then we are modeling good behaviors for our children that they will hopefully do for themselves. I'm seeing this come full circle with my own children, hearing them say they want to eat better because it makes them feel better, things like that. The concept of letting go is such a profound mindset change that it changes everything in your life. I've noticed changes in my husband too. It has made a difference in being able to step outside our comfort zone. When you are going through this kind of thing with your child, it can get really lonely.

I've shifted my speech therapy focus to teens instead of younger children. I'm able to do executive function coaching with the teens and have the parents help them. I'm able to bring my understanding of how the brain functions and also bring my speech education into play too. I've reached the point where I really enjoy waking up in the mornings and don't want to go to bed at night because I love what I'm doing. I would describe it as joyful because I'm serving people. Not that I wasn't serving people before, but I'm finally serving in a way I truly love. I feel like I'm making a difference in people's lives. I've become a touch person in the community for support. We've dealt with everything from mental health to substance abuse to homelessness, potential sex trafficking, foster care, and gender and sexuality issues.

If there's one thing I would say to people reading this book, it would be to join the HBR group.
You've already bought the book, but what you're
missing out on is the relationships and collabo-
rations with the people in Martha's community.
I've learned so many things I didn't think I would
ever learn, from technology to marketing. It's
such a joy to work in a space of such possibility
and help others versus just punching a time card.
We're all just trying to do the best with the cards
we've been dealt. When you surround yourself
with a community that lifts you up and challenges
you beyond what you thought you were capable
of is when you really see the results. It inspires
you to take the next step, to share insights, and
to support each other. The opportunity now is
enormous, but you need to have a community of
people behind you that will lift you up and help
you realize your true potential. That is what HBR
is. It really kept me afloat during the pandemic.
People were checking in with me, asking how I was

holding up. It was my perfect timing to have this to focus on.

My long-term goals are to be able to speak publicly to mom groups and to school administrations about the importance of mental health over academics, and to be able to support teenagers who are really struggling by helping them understand what's going on with their brains and how they can get back to more normalcy and maintain or restore connection with their family. My greatest desire is to see families stay connected by doing the various things I set up for them.

This past year has been all about reconnection: reconnecting to my family, reconnecting to my field, and reconnecting to myself.

When TV Came Calling

I got an email one night. Mike, my husband, and I were watching a couple shows before we went to bed. It's like our decompression time. We were sitting on the couch, and an email came in. I thought it was spam. It was this person saying they were an executive producer for a reality show that focused around business for good and creating good in the world. And I was like, *If this is spam, it's really good spam, right?* And so I responded.

I really wasn't sure if it was one of those scams—you know, the Nigerian royal family—informing me that I just inherited $40 million.

But I took a chance, I responded. I would love to do a reality show. And especially one whose slogan is "four days to save the world!" I got the email, I read through it, I was like, *I'm responding.* I didn't even send it to my publicist or anything. I responded myself: *Okay, I'm down. What do we do next? When do we talk? What's going on?* They emailed me back and set up an appointment to talk the very next day. We were fifteen minutes into talking and the executive producer said, "We don't even need to talk anymore. Do you want to do this?" I didn't have to think hard about that. "I'm in . . . like, yesterday. I NEED to do this." So we're filming in June.

I'm sure they found me because I was just doing the HBR stuff. Because I do HBR stuff all day, every day.

The message for anyone reading this is: Don't worry so much about "Will I get a reality TV deal?" Just do you, do your thing, and really enjoy doing that day in and day out. Make a good business, help lots of people, and the right people will find you. Oh, and use the HBR strategy, of course. Because let's call it—that's where the gold is.

Writing a Book

You're now reading this book. And through the creation of this book, that whole world opened up in a different way.

Like so many people I had an Achilles' heel of even getting this book done in the first place. Just getting off the starting line was difficult. I had some personal development I needed to go through in order to even start. It's okay to get a little paralyzed every once in a while. But once the book was done, I worked with my publicist to gauge some interest. I can't remember exactly how it happened. But anyway, a publisher said, "Okay, so we really like this. Not only do we really like this, but we want to do a four-book deal (well, it's a three-book deal with them having first right of refusal for the fourth), and make Martha a household name."

And they are so gracious in that their intent is to make me a household name but with my integrity intact. It's a win-win, win-win, win situation. I didn't have to negotiate away who I am or how I show up in the world; they wanted me for me. And they said that what was different about me is that I'm authentic, that I'm transparent, and that I just show up as who I am, which is also what I teach in HBR. How to BE YOU the best way possible.

As you're reading this you may be thinking, *How big can my dreams get?* The fact is that whatever path you go down, whether you decide to write a book, whether you want to go and do a documentary, or whatever it is, there is a demand for your insight, there's a demand for your wisdom, there's a demand for you being you.

And when you go down these tracks, what you're really doing is just putting a flag out there saying "This is me." And, again, people will find you.

Most people writing a book are actually thinking fairly small, and initially I was thinking this book would be really great for my people. So I might just self-publish this and get it out there through my own platforms, which is an incredibly successful strategy for many, many people. But that next level is once you start to get a little bit of movement, once you start to get some momentum, all sorts of other opportunities will open up for you.

Marshall Goldsmith, who is a prolific professional development author and executive development coach who's written more than thirty-five books, often says that if you can get five thousand people to be interested in your book, you've got an audience, and you've got an audience that a publisher will be interested in.

So that's just another reason for you to continue to build your community, for you to continue to help people because your book can be that next level and can actually go to quite an extreme level. So now instead of selling five thousand copies of your book, wouldn't it be cool if you sold a couple of million?

CHAPTER THREE

The Three Pillars of a Home-Based Revolution

We need to create a business and income streams. We need to grow your mindset around how to do that through the business pillar. Many people try this and experience no growth or really struggle with their business. When you don't get the business right, it is a constant stress, so we are going to talk about getting it right for massive organic growth.

Next, we need to create communities. The core of all of this is creating audiences, attracting the right people, and understanding how to do that. Sometimes when people do this, they can feel overwhelmed by negativity and lack of trust. Some people may have attracted an audience but not the right one for them.

Finally, we need to understand who your tribe is, so you're attracting the right people.

For most people, when they have a go at this, they don't experience growth. They have the business, and it's just a struggle. When you don't get the business right, and when there is no growth or low growth, it's just constant stress. And that just isn't sustainable.

When you get the business pillar and the communities pillar right, this is where you can generate time. When you get the communities pillar and the attracting-the-right-people pillar right, you can have a profound impact on your world.

The Business Pillar

Many people just starting at business do a mockingbird thing. They see somebody else with a business, think they like what they're doing, and want to do that too. That's a natural response.

That's what I did. I was working at my corporate gig and talking to these business owners with digital marketing agencies. A lot of them weren't super bright. Whenever I talked to them, I asked, "You're selling this for how much?" and I was telling them how to do everything right. They were in essence ripping people off and didn't even know how to provide competent service.

That's why I decided to create my own marketing agency. But a business is like an iceberg. You see this small part at the top, but you don't see all of the moving pieces underneath. With the marketing agency, it was great, and I could deliver really well. It did not take me long to hit the squeeze point where I had to bring somebody else in. Now we're talking expenses, and I set my prices before I figured these new expenses. So I had to raise my prices. Never a fun thing to have to do, but it was necessary.

Then I ended up changing models because I didn't like how things worked. Some things worked, others didn't.

We had a team of independent contractors, but we got so busy handling small website changes that I just had enough. I basically wanted someone else's business.

I wanted what someone else did. That was my first mistake.

Who are your people and how do you want to serve them?

The first thing I should have done was go within and see how I wanted to serve. I should have asked, "Who are my people and how do I want to serve them?" That's not what I did. I asked, "Okay, how can I go make money?" (Puhleeeze do not do this.)

Now, did I make money? Yes. Did it feel great? No, it didn't. It was exhausting. It was probably more exhausting than my corporate job. Did I have freedom? Yes, kind of. But I was also tethered to my email. Always. We went to Disney World, but I still had to deal with some client stuff while I was there. Is that freedom? No. No, it's not.

In that first iteration, I traded in one form of slavery for another. It was a step up in my journey; it taught me a lot, but it was exhausting.

For most people, when they first start out, they're modeling what they do on what someone else does.

And while success does leave clues, what they're seeing is the tiny bit of the iceberg above the water, the success point. What they're not seeing is the enormous amount of work that goes on under the waterline, just like an iceberg.

Next, I started teaching women entrepreneurs how to do all this stuff. I taught sales funnels back in 2016. I taught email marketing and even partnered with GoDaddy at one point. We held an event and GoDaddy bought all the tickets which was awesome, but I just taught them everything. Like imagine the biggest fire hose ever. Now try to drink from it. It was an insane amount of information.

What I learned was people aren't ready for that kind of fire hose. "Women entrepreneurs" wasn't enough of a niche to be able to say, "Here's how you're going to do all of these different things." They came out over-whelmed because I told them everything I know, and I know this stuff inside and out. But I was teaching it using the lingo, and they couldn't anchor it with their own specific businesses, so even though I was spitting gold that day, they couldn't digest it—so it essentially didn't matter.

Next, I went into people's businesses and got them to a point where they knew what they were offering and who they were offering it to. That was the breakthrough point, because nothing else matters. I can teach you the "how to do this" and "how to do that," but none of it matters if you don't know who you're talking to, what you're offering them, or if that is even a viable business.

It's not even just knowing who that person is and what you're offering them; it's deeper than that.

It's

- **Are you here to serve that person?**

- **How do you want to serve that person?**

It's that deep. A lot of women entrepreneurs came to my events at the same place I was when I started the digital marketing agency: "I want to make money." We need to address some things first before we can get into all of that. Those are the things that mattered. Once we get those things squared away, then we can get specific about what we need to do.

We need to get a group set up,

we need to be able to attract them to the group,

we need to be able to train them and help them transform in one way or another, and

we need to work out how you can help them transform.

There are all of these things they can't begin to get into until they know who the heck their person is. That is not just a "client, a dream client, or a client avatar thing." It is more service-based than that and focuses on who you are and how you are going to serve your people.

Victim Mentality

First of all, people need to address their mindset and whether they are harboring a victim mentality. Victim mentality doesn't make you a bad person, and it can be addressed, but it is something we need to self-identify if that is what we are doing.

Victim mentality is an issue because we are focusing on what has happened to us. We focus on "this happened, and then this happened, and then oh my gosh, this happened," and we end up sounding like we are complaining. What we are really focusing on is what happened to us. When we are focused on what has happened or what is happening, we're not focused on creating anything, because we can only focus on one thing at a time.

If you are focusing on what is annoying you or who wronged you, you can't turn and look at the things you want to create in your life. We need to address if that is what you are looking at, because if you are, we need to shift over to what you want to create in your life, otherwise you can't grow; you're paralyzed. And the worst part is—it's you. You paralyzed yourself with the choices you made and how you chose to see life.

It can be difficult because we seem to develop muscle memory in our brains. Once that memory is created, it requires a lot of snapping back that rubber band. It requires catching yourself in the moment. It can be tiring to focus on it for so long, but the good news is that it only takes a couple of weeks, then after that you will be where you need to be. Sometimes you will slip back into the victim mentality, but you will feel it because it won't feel as good. Then you will know how to move yourself out of it. Seems easy enough, right? Go ahead, try it!

Emily Cleghorn
FROM TEACHER TO PINTEREST ENTREPRENEUR

I was on maternity leave, dreading the idea of going back to work. I had been trying to grow my business, but it wasn't really going anywhere. I didn't know where I was going to find the things that I needed to get it off of the ground.

I contacted my school division and told them I wasn't going to be coming back. I was a second-grade teacher and I enjoyed it, but it wasn't my passion. The socialization was nice, building relationships with my students was nice, but there was a lot I dreaded about it. I actually missed my

Photo by Christine Friesen Photography

firstborn's first steps because I was at work. My husband took a video of it and sent it to me, and I just stood there in my classroom and cried. I wasn't supposed to miss that.

It was heartbreaking.

Until I met my husband, I didn't want kids. I didn't have a long-term goal. I was going to be a teacher and just work until retirement. After that, I didn't know what was going to happen. I was quite passive.

After I met my husband and we had our daughter, we started dreaming of creating a life of self-sustainability. We wanted to live closer to family. Right now, we live 5,600 kilometers away from them. We knew that the only way that we were going to be able to move back home and be closer to our families was if we created our own business so that we didn't have to rely on the job market on the East Coast of Canada.

Where we were living the job prospects weren't good at all. The salary gap between a teacher in

Alberta and a teacher in Nova Scotia where I'm from is a \$30,000 or more difference. My husband works in the forestry industry and that is monopolized by one company. If that company doesn't like you, then your chances, like ours, are slim. They control how much they pay you.

The salaries on the East Coast are significantly lower than what we're being paid in Alberta. And we didn't want to rely on somebody else to make our dreams of living closer to family a reality.

I started my network marketing business and tried to get that off the ground. I tried, and I tried, and I tried. And I failed, and I failed, and I failed. I was missing a lot of business tools that I wasn't quite sure how to find. *And then I found Martha*. And everything flipped upside down. I went from failure to stability. I now know what I need to do, and I have the steps to do it.

So instead of being a billboard for someone else, which I didn't want to be for a network marketing company, I began seeing the possibilities for branding myself and helping people in a much bigger way. It went from just helping in one little, tiny aspect of my clients' lives to being able to help them on a larger scale.

I am a body, mind, and Pinterest business coach. My target market is entrepreneurial women who want to own their life, body, mind, and business. I help mom entrepreneurs who've had a rough childhood and now they're carrying around the post-baby baggage and weight. They might have health issues but they're not quite sure what's going on. They want to create financial freedom for their family so that they can watch their kids grow up.

I'm collecting all the tools and skills that I need so that I can help them with the mind aspect, the life aspect, and the nutrition/exercise aspect and then also growing their business on Pinterest, because that's where I've had a lot of success.

One of the big things for me was to understand how my traumatic childhood affected my mindset.

I was abused in many different ways and was carrying around the thought pattern that I wasn't good enough, that I didn't matter. I believed I was just a waste of space and nobody really cared for me or wanted to hear what I had to say.

But then I found my voice. I started dealing with the emotions that I had stored deep, deep down inside.

That really opened the doors up.

Then I discovered Pinterest.

Now, I had been a Pinterest user for years. I used it to find lesson plans and craft and quilting ideas.

When I discovered that I could use it for my business, my website went from crickets to a constant flow of traffic and leads within a matter of two to three months. I knew I needed to tell people about this because not a lot of people know how to use Pinterest for their business.

I created a course called Attracting Pinterest Users to Your Website and launched it. Right now I have about one hundred women working on using

Pinterest to grow their business. One of my students, who is big in the horse industry, messaged me unsure if "horse people" use Pinterest. I gave her reassurance they did, and within a couple days of her first pin, she had one hundred impressions (views/interactions). It's a massive platform that's way underutilized. Helping these women who are struggling with getting views on their platforms is so rewarding.

I have developed an introductory course that's all about attracting Pinterest users to your website. It's five or six modules and it takes you from setup all the way through and helps you become fluent with the Pinterest lingo and all of the aspects of the platform. I'm developing some deeper-dive courses and workshops to help business owners really get specific and optimize their results.

I also have a community of about two hundred women who are just starting to dip their toes in the Pinterest water. It's growing. In March, I'll be a speaker and an exhibitor at the fourth annual

Women Inspiring Women Conference where I will be sharing some concepts from my book.

There are three things that have had a big impact on me.

One, mindset matters more than anything.

Two, consistency is key.

Three, show up to serve people without expecting anything back in return. It tends to lead to good things coming back to you as well . . . in abundance.

When I found Martha, I was fed up and frustrated. Maybe a little depressed. And now . . . I don't even know how to put it into words. A year ago, we didn't know how we were going to achieve our dream of moving back to the East Coast. With what we've learned from Martha and what we're implementing, we've been able to buy a home on the East Coast. That will give us the abilities to have our farmstead. We'll be moving there in the spring.

And we won't have to rely on the traditional job market to provide for our family.

What I wish I'd known about before all of this is: Where I am in life isn't who I am in life. Not letting my outside circumstances define who I am and what I am able to do. I have a choice in how I handle situations. I can turn my pain into purpose. I can use it as a driving force instead of feeling chained down.

And that mindset makes the biggest difference. Without that, you have an anchor around your leg.

What I really want other women to know is: Whatever death somebody spoke over you as a child or as an adolescent was not true. It was a lie and had nothing to do with you; it was all about them. You can change the world if you choose to.

Scarcity or Abundance?

Another key mindset to overcome is that we are all competing with each other. I believe we are all here in symphony with each other for a reason and not to compete with each other. I have a Christian outlook that there is an ultimate enemy, and that is the root of competition. Now by contrast, I love collaboration. I love being able to work with other people's genius and serve, because at the end of the day, you have your people and there's no way you can be the only "be-all, end-all servant" for these people.

If you bring in what I call "super-friends," you can all serve these people together, and then your people get an excellent experience. Nobody has to feel weird. Nobody has to avoid each other at networking events, you know what I'm saying.

It can be a natural thing. We'll all go back to where we came from. We're not supposed to live in or work in these cubicles forty hours a week for these corporations. We came from tribes; we came from communities.

Everybody did something different. My husband calls this the *Star Trek* society, where nobody gets paid to do what they're doing. They're all doing what they do because they love doing it. You don't need to compete with people, you just collaborate, and you all serve just the same. There is no such thing as competition. Nobody holds exactly the same cards you hold. Nobody has the same experience you have. Nobody has the same background you have. Your flavor is your own, and there's not another human on the planet that has your flavor. By nature, there is no competition. There can't be; it's impossible.

Any competition created in your mind is exactly that—a scarcity mentality, which we're certainly taught in our education system and our economic system. We're taught there's only so much pie to go around, and we have to fight for our share of the pie. The reality is quite different. The reality is an abundance mentality. The more we help, the more we build, the more we both receive, and then the more we are able to give. It's a really virtuous cycle when we start to look at collaboration.

The people I work with who have the hardest time moving forward still end up moving forward—it just takes longer. These same people may have gone through other courses about the same kinds of things—building your business, building income streams—and they think they understand about email lists, but they are still not having success. Maybe they were taught by the same person, maybe by different people, but in this industry, what we see are echo chambers.

How do you build an email list? Echo chamber.

How do you build a website? Echo chamber.

How do you make a landing page? Echo chamber.

They learn these things but are disconnected from the whole. That is, How do these things work in relation to each other? That is where they get stuck.

I hope this isn't true, but it appears some coaches/consultants deliberately keep their people confused so they continue to need them and pay them. They learn all of these things separately and struggle to make them all work together. Because that is the secret sauce: getting them all to work together like a chain on a bike.

Whenever people start learning stuff from me they previously learned in bits and pieces, they have to unlearn some of it, because what they learned was a scarcity way of doing things. They learned things that make this person necessary for them forever. When I give them the entire strategy of how to work it all together, they have to unlearn the "other ways" in order to realize it can be very simple. It doesn't have to be that hard. Their mind is stuck in "This is supposed to be hard." The reason for that is because they've been fed a narrative of "This is really hard." And they believed it. But that doesn't make it true.

Surrender

A mindset of surrender is surrendering to the universe, surrendering to God, or whatever you want to call your Creator. I call it God. But it is a surrender to a bigger will than your own.

I felt like I was pushing a rock up a hill in everything I did. One day soon after a Women's Entrepreneur

Summit I did, I went in my bedroom, dropped to my knees, cried, and typed out all the thoughts screaming through my head.

I will do whatever you want. I no longer want the reins. I don't want to be the head of this thing. I don't want to be the brains of this operation. I want to live in service, and I want to be the hands and feet of God. I want to live in purpose and be able to do what my God wants to do here on the planet, and I want to be a conduit. I want to be a vessel.

I'm tearing up as I write, remembering it. I surrendered anything and everything I thought I knew.

"I'll just do what you want me to do. That's it. I get it. I'm done," I prayed.

It was the most freeing experience in my entire life. From that day on, I followed what I call Divinely inspired footsteps. I get a tap and a nudge. It says, "Martha, do this; Martha, do that." Until you surrender to your Creator, you can't feel those taps and nudges because you're attempting to lead the show. You're so busy up in your head, you can't tell when you're supposed to do this or supposed to do that. When you get into a place of surrender, you're being led. Divinely led.

Whenever you're being led, you're NOT in front. You can't follow from the front, if that makes sense. You can't be led if you're doing the leading.

Suddenly everything came easily. It's easy to serve your people once you surrender. Your people find you like they're magnetized to you. It's like they can't stay away. They just want to know more; then you create this really deep, meaningful, impactful community, and serve them. That's what life is about. Then we can build different income streams around it, not feeling skeezy or weird, because we're just in service. We're all just helping each other out. For me it got very, very easy.

Whenever you are being led, you're NOT in front. . . . You can't be led if you're doing the leading.

CHAPTER FOUR

Income Streams

The first thing I tell people to look at before we look at starting an income stream is: Who are you serving and how do you want to serve them? Typically, the people they are serving are themselves early in the journey, so how can you help them create a transformation?

People realize they have a course within them—to teach how they went through the transformation they experienced. That course can be monetized, and that is an income stream. You can write books and create business or an income stream around a book. You can have your affiliate marketing, which is really just lifestyle marketing the way I treat it.

Affiliate Marketing

Affiliate marketing should never be in your face. For example, you share a picture of this stroller and say, "Hey, we love the stroller, here's where we got ours." Then you leave a link there. That's the kind of affiliate marketing a lot of bloggers have used for years to build income. Affiliate marketing is more of a long game, because it's going to build up and build up and build up. But it's definitely something to do.

My suggestion to people looking at affiliate marketing is to walk around your house with either your voice recording on your phone or a notebook, and take note of the things you love and cannot live without. Then go and Google search them and the term *affiliate* and see if those products have affiliates. There are also Amazon affiliates.

When you sign up, they often ask a lot of questions you shouldn't be scared of. They are asking to ensure you are not a spammer or are not going to make them look bad. They will ask about your website and your audience. Then they will approve you or not. Sometimes they require a big audience, but it doesn't hurt to ask, and you can always try again later.

Some of my students approached people without an affiliate program and proposed it to them, saying they love what they do. There is nothing wrong with reaching out. The worst that will happen is you will look like you know what you are talking about and might be able to help them out with additional income.

Every time someone uses your link to buy one of their products, the seller or manufacturer gives you a commission. It's all tied in with your audience. The more you can build a community of people who love what you do, the more you can genuinely recommend and become affiliates with products and programs that serve your audience.

Build an Ongoing Stream

As you keep creating your content, you can put affiliate links not just in social media but also on your website, in your blog, on your YouTube channel, and places like that as well. A good idea is to do reviews of products, then just have an affiliate link. In the beginning when you are growing your presence, you may not see any traffic to the link. Later when more people are going to your website and going to your YouTube channel—maybe even in a year from now—they are going to click on that link. It will happen if you're consistent and you keep showing up in service to your community. If you keep showing up consistently, they will come, they will love you, and they will want to get everything you talk about, because by nature they will love it too.

I have people that devour my YouTube channel. They tell me they watch my videos all day and night, so much so their kids know my voice. They ask, "Is that Martha screaming again?" because I soapbox a lot on my videos, LOL . . . yes, it's a thing. When you build your community and are consistent, your tribe is going to want more. That can be difficult when you are starting out and it feels quiet, and that's okay. That's where everyone starts. The difference between being right there and having people just devouring your content is continuing to do it.

Oprah is the queen of affiliate marketing. Her magazine is filled with affiliate links. They are monetizing not just through subscription services but by offering free stuff online. You have to think why they offer free stuff online; it's because they're attracting their people, then serving up what their people would like.

Next look at *Cosmopolitan* magazine or any magazine and you will see a ton of affiliates. The next rank beneath that is bloggers or podcasters, which could be the same or different. If you look for a recipe on Google, you will see a good ninety affiliate links in one recipe. If you go on YouTube, look up a video on how to bake something and click on a link: that goes to a product that YouTuber is getting a small commission or a percentage of sales on. It's one of the best kept secrets of developing passive income streams.

Network Marketing

Network marketing is an income stream that is very polarizing. I don't think it's for everybody and freaks some people out, but if you give it a try, you can build a fantastic audience because you're building a team. As you're building that team, you're developing relationships with those people. That can become your very first community, then you can build your community out from that.

It's really great as long as the network marketing company you choose is in alignment with your ethics and values. Of course, you shouldn't choose something that isn't. But as long as the company is in line with your ethics, your values, your own passions, and what you enjoy, it can work wonders for you. For example, I couldn't do Pampered Chef, because everybody knows I don't cook. But for some people that love cooking and cooking is their passion, that is the way they serve their community, and Pampered Chef could then be a perfect fit for them.

Health and wellness are my thing because I love feeling good and keeping my family healthy with non-toxic stuff. I was with a network marketing company that was all about non-toxic products. That's just because that's my thing. And when people signed up through that company, I already knew they were my people. If they care about non-toxic products and that care was as deep-rooted for them as it was for me, we were connected on a level a lot of people were not.

The more "me too" connections we can have, the better. It is a bit like two pieces of Velcro. If we have one little "me too" connection, you are kind of connected. That's awesome. Then we find out there's something else we share. I have alcoholism in my background, so say they're a recovering alcoholic as well, we've got two "me too" things. If they have a six-year-old, we've got three, and now we're getting a solid connection. That's how you build that audience. Network marketing is a fantastic anchor point IF done well. I'm not going to drill down on it right now, but I revolutionized the entire industry in six months, so make sure you join my group at the end of the book if you're wanting to know how to do this without feeling like a skeezball.

Finding Your Niche

I started with my business strategist consulting where I worked directly with businesses, which I still do. Then I added course creation and group coaching and that's where I was able to directly affect thousands of families all over the world. That is where I found my people and felt like I started lighting up. It felt good to show up for these folks and show them the things I know.

This amplified my network marketing business as well as my business strategist business because I was able to light up there in that niche. That is why people say you have to find the right niche, and you have to niche down to really be successful, and it's true.

When you realize you are there to serve your community, it illuminates everything.

But no one tells you how to actually do it. After I started network marketing, I thought I would throw in this affiliate marketing as well. I thought, "Okay, we need this," then I would throw in an affiliate link. I would say, "I get a little bit of money off it, but I also actually use this, love it, and think you would love it," and then they click away.

I used to have that scarcity mentality. I thought I would put an affiliate link out there and they would find a way to click around it. It was probably some crab in a bucket years ago who helped me think like that! But when you realize you are there to serve your community, it illuminates everything. You begin to see different ways you can serve your community that you can layer over your business. For me, I found my favorite people through the network marketing industry, but it is really about being in alignment with the people you serve. That is when you start to look at things from a completely different perspective.

Meggan Larson
AUTHOR AND BUSINESS BUILDER

I was twenty-four years old when I first got the entrepreneurial bug. I sat in a room full of entrepreneurs, many of whom were succeeding, and it seemed simple enough. Read a script, close the deal. I spent the next thirteen years trying—and

Photo courtesy of Meggan Larson

failing—to attain the success that so many others had achieved. I spent over $30,000 on my business education only to come away with very little to show for it.

Right before I met Martha Krejci and started her signature program, HBR, I was on the verge of a nervous breakdown. I was working forty to sixty hours a week making about $3.45 per hour when it was all said and done, my kids had stopped asking me to read to them because I was always too busy, and I was so stressed out that I was actually concerning medical professionals.

I knew Martha was different from the very first time I heard her speak. She was teaching people how to lead authentically from their hearts, and I could hardly believe it. I had been told that it was impossible to succeed that way. That I had to be completely duplicitous and couldn't lead from my heart or I would fail. Here was this multimillionaire telling me that she builds her businesses without chasing people down for the close, without pressuring her friends to support her, and by leading with what's most important to her.

I jumped all the way into her world and began creating income streams literally out of thin air. I don't have a college or university degree; all I had was a deep desire to serve people from my heart and make a lot of money doing it. She told me that was all I needed, and I believed her.

I can hardly believe the life I get to live now. I'm creating courses, coaching people in ways I never imagined, collaborating with some of the coolest people on the planet, and I've even become a published author. I have made more money in the last four months than I had in the last three years combined. My husband has been able to retire from backbreaking work and he gets to stay home to homeschool our kids. I have more time to spend with my family, and I no longer worry about making ends meet. In 2019, we were so broke that we had to sell everything we owned just to be able to buy paint to sell our house. Less than a year later, I was making enough money to bring my husband home full-time, cover our sponsor child's unexpected monthly medical expenses, and support organizations in ways I had only dreamed of doing before.

My dreams are expanding daily. I've finished writing my second book and am already on to writing the third, while simultaneously creating more courses, increasing my coaching clientele, and encouraging others to pursue their dreams. When I met Martha, I didn't believe that any of this could be possible, and I certainly didn't believe in myself. She had enough faith in me for both of us, and through her leadership, my entire family line has been transformed. My birth father has jumped in and gone from worrying he would die alone and unloved to someone who inspires people daily and is no longer worried about making enough money to get by. My ten-year-old daughter and I are coauthoring a children's book, and my sons get to see their mom succeeding wildly on the couch beside them.

The most important thing I've learned is that all you need to succeed is a desire to serve people in an authentic way. When I used to hear the word *entrepreneur*, I pictured myself having to make hundreds of cold calls each day, reading a script I didn't write, and trying to manipulate people into working with me. That felt gross and I didn't want to do it, but I didn't know of any other way to make enough money to fulfill the dreams in my heart. When I think of the word *entrepreneur* now, I picture thousands of men and women linking arms and bringing others along to success with them.

If I could send a message out to millions of others it would be this: The dreams in your heart were placed there for a reason. All you need to succeed is a desire to serve as authentically you and believe in yourself. If you have those things, you'll be unstoppable. If you have those things, you'll change not only your world but the world of those around you too.

CHAPTER FIVE

Creating
Communities

When I first tried online advertising and creating the funnels everyone was teaching, I realized while you could technically do it, you need to have a huge wallet (think $10,000 per month) to build your business that way. But if I built a community, and nurtured and served that community, it was a better way forward for me.

Serving your community is giving away trainings and other free things, then allowing them to move down the rabbit hole if they feel it is necessary for them. Serving your community is not spending $300 a day on Facebook ads and wondering if it will work or not; it is spending thirty minutes doing a free training, giving them a call to action, and having people moving down the pipeline that way. It is not only a better way to procure clients but you end up having a longer relationship with those clients.

It is not like they just buy something and leave—they buy something and stay. They stay for the next thing and the next thing and the next thing, because they love you at that point, and you love them right back. You've built a relationship with them. You can't do that without a community.

You don't want everyone in your community though, which sometimes we don't realize until they are there and it feels like work having them there. We are not supposed to work with everybody on the planet. We're supposed to help OUR people. But whenever we attract the wrong people, it is usually via the wrong message or by trying to be somebody we're not. When you attract the wrong people, you have to continue to be that person who attracted that individual. That is hard work since it wasn't you in the first place. If they're not your people, they will hold you to a standard that is not comfortable for you and isn't what you were even offering in the first place. And a lot of times they're going to be problematic and have bad expectations. Just don't do it. Be you. Be gloriously you.

Your Bat Signal

I refer to finding your zone of genius and articulating it to attract the right people as the bat signal. It is the part of yourself you send into the sky. People will then come swarming to you because you are speaking their language and your truth.

I have given many bat-signal workshops and trainings and it sometimes takes hours for people to really drill down, but the key questions to ask are:

- **Where were you three years ago?**

- **What was your life like?**

I do a sort of three-year regression with people and sit in the moment of three years ago.

110

"So, you're on your couch. What house are you sitting in? What job do you have? Are you happy in that job? Is it paying the bills? Are you stressed out? If you're stressed, name the things that are stressing you out. What are you scared of? What are you hopeful for? What are your dreams? What are your main goals and objectives right there? What do you think of when you think, *If ONLY I knew how to* . . . What is the end of that sentence?

You drill all the way down on who you were as a person, which is actually easier to do with hindsight being 20/20. Look back three years and define yourself as a person and that is who you're serving.

Then create ways to share the transformations you had between then and now. You are not the same person you were three years ago. You can help other people like you bridge that gap. If you are worried it is not much of a transformation—don't. If it was too big a transformation, people won't believe they can do it anyway. Keep the transformation nice and succinct and give them benchmarks on how they can get there.

Your best bat signal is you, earlier in your journey.

Your best bat signal is you, earlier in your journey.

Getting fitter, losing weight, overcoming a hurdle, or building a business may not feel like that big a deal at the moment. But looking from the outside in, what you have done is actually something many people would love to have some real, on-the-ground insight into how to do themselves.

What we do in HBR (Home-Based Revolution) the first week is all about mindset, which continues throughout, but we don't do anything until we fully understand how valuable we are as people first. Then we do the digging about what we have to offer. At that point, you're already peeling off the layers of society telling you you're lacking this and lacking that and therefore needing the things they are trying to sell. That is a whole societal thing, but it has made people feel they are not good enough. We are not born this way; it is a nurture thing.

Working with mindset is neuroplasticity—we rewire the brain to create things instead of finding reasons why people don't want what we have or finding reasons why we are not valuable. It is a total shift. There are times when it still comes up, but within the community they support each other and show each other their worth, which is a really cool thing.

We don't put out our bat signal unless we are confident. When a bat signal goes up, it is because help is on the way. It goes up to say, "I'm a lighthouse; come to me, I got you." We are teaching people to help.

It means there is a need for more people to understand your transformation and join you on your journey. The bat signal is a metaphor for everyone reading this book to say you can help people, you can find what it is and start projecting it out there.

FINDING YOUR NICHE

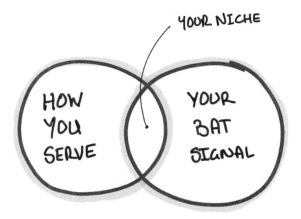

YOUR NICHE

HOW YOU SERVE

YOUR BAT SIGNAL

Being specific about how you serve is only part of the Puzzle. Your Bat Signal, or who you serve, is the other half.

You need to understand who you help and what you help them achieve for a strong Niche.

Uncovering
Your Superpower

Your superpower is usually the thing you do every day that is so inherent in your life, you don't think twice about it. It is something you just do.

Tricks to uncover this are:

Carry a notebook with you.

Keep track of the questions people ask you, and at the end of each week, read those questions and see if there's a trend for what people are really asking for.

People from the outside will see your superpower and respond to it before you realize what it is. People are asking about it, but you don't think about it because it comes naturally.

Be Mindful
in the Moment

This is work to begin with but worth it once you have the muscle memory for doing it. Pay attention to how you feel when you talk about things. When you hit your superpower, your entire demeanor will change. You will get excited and can talk about it for hours. You want to drill down on this, and that is your superpower.

I was talking to a client about finding her superpower. She was talking about what it could be but in a very methodical, data-driven way that was very dry.

Then she started talking about what it *might* be, and everything lit up. Her whole demeanor changed, and she glowed. Then she started talking about another subject. After I asked her a couple of questions to make sure, I saw her demeanor change again and that was the best signal of her superpower.

It's about feeling excited, feeling bubbly, and loving and wanting to support and share that thing.

It's about feeling excited, feeling bubbly, and loving and wanting to support and share that thing. You could do it twenty-four hours a day if you wanted. If you feel drained and like it is a drag, it is probably not your superpower.

Superpower Examples

I have a client who works with kids who are dyslexic. Her own kids are extremely dyslexic and also have extreme learning disabilities, so through the years she developed some hacks and tricks to help parents work with their kids in a way not available in a system anywhere. That's a superpower of hers.

I have another client who was adopted. She works with adoptees through their emotional trauma from abandonment. I have two clients who teamed up and work with mental disabilities within families. They work with teens with depression and anxiety, because both of them had some traumatic things happen with their kids. They have a perception or point of view most people don't. They honor their kids in the process, work with them, and end up with a solid situation. They make apps now and are doing all sorts of cool stuff together.

There are a couple of authors who write books together. They also come from a background of trauma and started a group to support people in creating the lives they desire on the other side of trauma.

These people are picking up very heavy things. They don't have to be heavy. It is about using your experiences to serve the collective. The way they earn income is showing up in service to help someone move along their path. It makes all the stuff they have been through not just something that happened to them but something that is now fueling them to serve others. If it hadn't happened, they wouldn't have had that experience, and they wouldn't be able to help.

Many people have a multi-view perspective on issues. For example, for the medical thing, doctors will have a perspective, or if it is a school thing, the schools will have a perspective, but that is not always the whole picture. When you have a lived experience and are teaching others about it, you get that intersection of what people normally hear, plus a little dose of real experience of what you did to overcome.

There are people who help with websites, social media, Pinterest, and other things they struggled to understand. There are others helping with diet, weight loss, and getting healthy. They are less focused on how you are not enough and more focused on getting our bodies healthy. They focus on getting bodies healthy, getting to know you, then the weight comes off naturally, as opposed to the industry which touts losing sixty pounds in five days. They are saying to their communities, "Listen, I'm not perfect right now. I'm fifty pounds down from what I was last year. I'm a mom, I'm busy, and this is what I'm doing. I'm here—join me on this journey."

There are doctors and chiropractors I work with who usually do body work or consultations. They learn they can also create other income streams. For example, some massage therapists teach your significant other how to massage for pain reduction at home for a fee.

The Bat Signal Is a Journey

The thing about the bat signal is that it's a journey; it's not as if a light bulb suddenly turns on and there's your bat signal, and that's it for the rest of your life.

One of my HBR members thought she had her bat signal down and knew how she was going to serve. But as she began to develop communities, she found that it didn't inspire her as much as she thought it would; she was reluctant to really go all in. In fact she was kind of bored with it. She reported that it felt like work . . . that means she didn't have it, that's not it. If it feels like work, it's not it. It should feel like *Oh my gosh, I just started this thing. I have to tell everyone I thought of this thing, I have to share it.* And once she made a tiny change to her bat signal, like just a degree change, all of a sudden she started showing up every day.

Now I see her talking on her public feed about what she does, like she is in it; she owns her space now. But she just had to get right into it and tweak it. I think she tweaked it maybe three or four different times. And the last time that she tweaked it, she even stepped away for three weeks or so just to try to take a pause and figure out what was going on. And that's where she switched it just a little bit, and then it just blew the doors off.

The lesson in that is when you're working on this bat signal, don't be too hard on yourself. If it isn't perfect up front, that's okay. This is an evolution. What's most important is that you're in motion, you're actually giving it a go, you're working on it. Know that the bat signal that you come up with today may not be the absolute pinnacle of your final bat signal. The evolution is really important. And you'll know you're on the right path when you get a little teary when you think about it or suddenly there's fireworks going off in your mind about what you can do with this.

＼ ｜ ／

One of the most amazing experiences—if you ever go to the world-famous Galleria dell'Accademia in

Italy—is viewing Michelangelo's sculpture *David*. The more powerful experience is that the whole way up to the *David* statue is seven or eight half-finished sculptures by the master. It's a moving experience because you see these extraordinary sculptures emerging from incredibly rugged marble. They're in different stages of evolution; some are nearly finished, and some are just started. You can see an arm of one and the beginning of a torso of another. As you see the figures emerging from a rugged rock, you begin to see this genius emerge. And then right at the end of the hall is this unbelievable sculpture of *David*, which is breathtaking in real life.

When I think of starting with somebody's first bat signal, it's sort of like the big rock that *David* was sculpted from. It was chipped away from a rugged piece of marble, just as the half-finished statues were. Your first bat signal can just be the rock, and then you can chip away and create your own version of the *David* statue. It's important that you have the rock to begin with—you have to start somewhere to be able to chip away at it.

Along the way, you're chipping out a little bit of marble, you're refining that marble. Some of the strokes on the marble are big hammer strikes, and some of them are refined with sandpaper. The analogy I'm wanting you to understand is that the statue of *David* didn't happen overnight. It came from marble, and if all you find right now is the block of marble that you're going to carve your statue from? That's okay. Just put your block of marble on the platform. It all starts right there.

Sheri Poyant
A RECOVERING PERFECTIONIST

Life is so much different than even two or three years ago. About three years ago I left my full-time, very stressful job. My mom had just passed away from Alzheimer's, and I was getting sick from the amount of stress from my job and family life. My son was being bullied, and I was feeling so torn about not being able to be home for him after school. It all took a toll on me. I ended up with depression, anxiety, and physical illness. My family made the decision for me to leave my job so I could heal. It was during this time that I started looking into working for myself. I'd always wanted to do this. My first degree from college was in textiles, fashion, merchandising, and design. I always thought I would own my own business. I've always had this entrepreneurial spirit but had no idea how

Photo courtesy of Sheri Poyant

to implement it. Everyone always told me I'd never make any money being an entrepreneur.

I was working as a teacher in a very stressful situation, my health was not great, my mom had died. It triggered a lot of things in my life that made me really think there had to be something better than this. My parents both died at an early age. My dad was sixty-six and my mom was in her early seventies. I've always had the philosophy to have fun while you're living. I didn't want to be that person at seventy-five years old finally able to have a chance to live their life. My anxiety and depression and autoimmune issues just left me feeling awful.

It was daunting.

I was at the point where I didn't even want to go on anymore because I was so sick and tired of feeling this way. I felt like I wasn't present for my family. Working full-time as a woman is really difficult because you feel torn in so many directions. You want to do well at whatever you're doing, but something always gives and it's really stressful for a working mom.

I had to make a change.

As I began in this journey of running my own business, I had a clear idea of what I wanted to do. I was helping women who are fifty and fabulous, but it wasn't specific enough. I wanted to help other women who were in my position: in their fifties, recovering from anxiety and depression, had autoimmune issues. Martha really helped me to drill down exactly who it was I wanted to help. At the end of the day, it was me, three years ago. It was that mom who was crying in her car going to work, feeling so stressed and drained and torn. That's when everything changed, and the light lit up for me.

I felt good. I felt like I had a purpose. I've always been a teacher, but now I'm teaching something different. I'm teaching people health and wellness and how to gain energy. I felt really great that I could help people, but it was still all over the place.

I didn't have that specific person in mind; it was just every woman that was fifty.

I'm writing a book on letting go of perfection, embracing the mess, and finding your balance. I'm also creating a signature course that goes along with the book. My plans are to be able to hold one-day workshops, as well as weekend retreats, so that I can share the principles in my book in person with other women. I also became an Oola life coach and am certified in their financial program as well. I have courses to help women be at a healthy weight and effectively create meal plans. I also have an Etsy store and a couple of network marketing avenues. I probably have about seven different things that are going on at any given moment.

It is so nice to have direction and know where I'm going. All of the pieces are starting to fall into place. The great thing about it is every single thing I'm doing all works cohesively together because I've been focused on who I'm helping. In terms of the business side of it, it is beginning to develop multiple streams of income for me. There is still more that I am creating, but I'm getting more of a social media presence. People are noticing me more, and I have more people coming into my lead group.

The first lesson I learned is to not speak to a big audience; speak to one person. That person is you at the beginning of this journey. That helps you really focus on solutions for that person and what their needs are and how you can help them. My bat signal evolved. It was almost like coming out of a tunnel into the light to see all sorts of new possibilities.

It was a process going through HBR, working with Martha on bat signal, and then working with Brett on writing a book. All of a sudden, I had this "aha moment" that who I needed to help was me, three years ago, and I wanted to help this woman find balance and turn her dreams into reality.

In order to do that, first you've got to kind of embrace the mess and let go of the perfection. I am a recovering perfectionist.

I've realized you don't have to do everything perfectly; you just have to get things done. Joy comes when you let some things go. That's what's been so wonderful about teaching other women. With HBR, it's not just Martha; it's the entire community. She leads us wholeheartedly, and as a community, we are going to change the world.

My bat signal evolved and changed and that's when the different streams of income made sense. I became a life coach to help people find balance. I started writing a book. From the book came workshops and retreats. I sell merchandise. I'm creating courses and signature programs. I'm putting my whole heart into my groups because that's what Martha does for us: she has taught us to give with our hearts and it'll come back to you tenfold.

It's important to allow your bat signal to change. As a recovering perfectionist, it was difficult to not snap my fingers and arrive immediately at my true signal. But people change and evolve, and your bat signal can change and evolve with you.

You've got to find your pain point—the point where it makes you cry because you realize that other people are hurting just like you were. You don't have to be the expert; you just have to be willing to help from your life experiences. Just know there is somebody out there who could benefit from knowing what you know.

The amazing part about my book is that it will resonate with you whether you're in your thirties or your seventies. It's an amazing feeling being able to help the people closest to me. What is even better is being able to help people I haven't even met yet. When you narrow down and focus on helping one person, you end up being able to help a bigger audience.

If I could say one thing to the people in my past who said I'd never make any money being an entrepreneur, it would be this: it's all about mindset. Going from a fixed mindset to one of growth is vital.

It's called neuroplasticity. The way we talk to ourselves is so important. If you think you're not going to make any money or be successful, then that's what's going to happen. But when you have a great coach who shows you a different way of thinking, anything becomes possible. My husband is now selling his drawings and has created an activewear line, and my sixteen-year-old son has monetized his YouTube channel. It all goes to show that anything is possible.

You're always going to be surrounded by well-meaning people who think they're protecting you by telling you to get a safe job to fall back on. What they don't know is that the opportunities for a more flexible life are endless and available to everyone. If you're reading this book, feeling encouraged that you too can have this abundant life, the best thing you can do is become part of Martha's Home-Based Revolution. Martha is so heart-centered and inspiring. Her community is an army of women and men who are going to make the world a more positive place. You'll get the support you need and have cheerleaders all along the way. Don't hesitate; just go for it!

Finding Your Ideal Audience

The person you are talking to is literally at the beginning of your journey three years ago (this is an arbitrary point in time, but I have found three years ago is where a lot of people started their journey). Where was the beginning for you? You are leading these people through a transformation. There is a point A. You have to think about what you were like at point A. Then you're leading them to point B.

Point A is where you're speaking to them. That is the person that whenever you speak directly to them, they will get the message right between the eyes. The common misconception is that if I only talk to this person, I'm leaving everyone else out and I'm never going to be successful. But whenever we talk to everybody, we are talking to precisely no one. No one is going to get it.

No one is going to read your words and wonder how you knew what they were thinking. You have to speak directly to the person you were sitting on the couch three years ago. Speak directly to their fears, hopes, and dreams. Then they will know you get them, and they will trust you immediately.

You are saying you were there, now you're here, and you can call out exactly where they are at right at that moment. They will automatically trust you can get them here. It is critical to speak the language they need to hear and answer their questions about the problems they have better than they can articulate themselves.

Creating Your Community

I start by creating Facebook groups, but you need ways congruent to Facebook in case something happens to Facebook and you lose your community. (Don't worry, I talk about all of this stuff in my free Facebook group Heart-Centered + Successful Work at Home Moms, feel free to join if you want.)

How Much Content Should I Have in My Group before I Start Inviting People?

Do not invite people! You want them to arrive organically. You don't just want people in your group; you want the right people in your group,. The number of people in your group is a vanity metric and does not matter.

For the first few people in your group, just to feel like you have some warm bodies there, you can ask family and friends to pop over and check it out because you are trying to grow it and need it to look like there are people there. They will join and that is no big deal. Do not do this past the beginning stage.

The only thing you need is a welcome video to set the expectations for what the group is about, a first training in the units section; this sets up what they can expect from you.

Don't go in guns-a-blazin' saying you will do five posts a day if that's not sustainable for you.

You also need to work out what is sustainable for you. That could mean a training every week, but don't go in guns-a-blazin' saying you will do five posts a day if that's not sustainable for you because you will look flighty. You will lose trust because you are not doing what you said you would do.

In my Facebook groups, I organize my content in the units section, so members can quickly and easily see the trainings or challenges I did in the past. When someone new comes to the group and wants to learn what you are talking about, they can go to your library (units section). You only need to have one training and a welcome video. My main training is my 90 Days Side Gig to Main Gig Challenge in unit 2 of my group, then you can check out allllll of the other trainings in the units section as well. Feel free to model after my setup; I'm here to help. Don't overthink this. Really. Don't do it.

I sometimes ask questions to make sure people are in the right spot. For example, my group is Heart-Centered + Successful Work at Home Moms on Facebook. I ask them, "Are you a work at home mom, or do you desire to be?" This makes sure they are in the right place.

Some people ask for their email addresses, but I don't recommend that. One of the reasons they go to our free Facebook group is because the barriers to entry are so low, they feel safe. It is like if you are at the mall browsing a store and someone comes and asks you to put your email address into something before you can continue browsing. I am going to leave the store. You can ask but understand there will be a percentage of people who don't come back to the group. This is a silly way to lose leads.

There is a strategy to get their emails once they're in the group, but it will feel better for them and you. You can offer a freebie or lead magnet. Possibly a guide, worksheet, or video on something. It needs to be something more than what you're teaching in the units section. Perhaps you can make an introductory training video for your Facebook group, then an in-depth training video that requires an email address to access right away. Then you can get them on an email list and continue to nurture them and add value outside of Facebook. (I teach this way more in depth in HBR.)

Free Facebook Groups vs Facebook Groups for Paying Clients

Our paying client groups are where we deliver material and support them through the process. We have Q&As, we have "lives," we have momentum calls where we do group coaching. There is far greater access to me and other experts I bring in. Everything is recorded and placed in the units section so people can go back and watch the old calls and binge on personal development.

Your free Facebook groups are for lead generation so there is less access. There are still plenty of trainings that should help your people out; they just don't go as deep as your course.

You can build websites and try other platforms, but they tend to be more disconnected. When it comes to building a community, social media is king.

CHAPTER SIX

Attracting the Right People

When I first started my boutique marketing business, I went to chambers of commerce, did workshops at other events, and talked about my zone of genius. That is how I found my business.

Would I do the same again? Not exactly. I was still asking where I was getting my money from, and I wasn't asking who I wanted to work with. Asking where the money is isn't necessarily going to get you the life you want.

If I had to do it over, I would ask what kind of businesses I want to serve, reach out to them, and ask them what's going on in their current experience. What is going on with their website, their leads, their growth, and start a conversation with them. Then hopefully I could offer something they were missing—or I could do better—but also build a community of those people online and do trainings to prove I know what I am talking about.

I would have niched down and put my bat signal out to the entire English-speaking world, then brought everyone into my group. Then I would make a post and say, "I'm taking on two clients this week. Who wants appointments?"

But I did it the hard way.

And now, thank goodness, you don't have to.

Organic Attraction vs Paid Attraction

Paid marketing is unnecessary. If you're going to use a paid marketing strategy, the only way I recommend is retargeting. That is, retargeting organic people you have already attracted.

A version of retargeting allows you to put an advertisement or message in front of someone who has already been to your sales page and didn't buy anything. You could put a discount or some other offer to get them off the fence, because they have already been to your sales page, so you know they are interested. There is a little bit of code that attaches to their computer address so when they are browsing other sites, the advertisers know to put up your advertisements because they have already visited your website.

Getting organic attraction doesn't cost money, but it does cost time. Will it take a lot of time? No.

Basically, you start showing up in different places online. Every day at 10 AM EST, Monday through Friday, I go live on my personal page, my business page, YouTube, and everywhere I can at once. I then get shared by people all over the place. Then everybody sees my content, and it is a good place to start for organic marketing because referral marketing is the best marketing there is.

It is "warm" because someone is suggesting you or their experience of you. You are not just showing up as a cold advertisement right in front of someone, leaving them to wonder who you are. They will keep scrolling regardless of whether you are their guide for what they are trying to do in their life. You might know your stuff and be a boss in your content, but they will never in their life know because they do not have a connection—it is just an ad.

That is where organic and authentic marketing come in. That is where you build relationships with people and they get to share you. In psychology, people love to be the reason someone else sees something really cool. If you said something brilliant and they share it, psychologically they are connected to the brilliance. When they share it, they are sharing your brilliance as well as their own because they are connected to it. It is the best thing ever! You are warm-delivered to their entire audience.

Organic attraction
doesn't cost money,
but it does cost time.

You can also do this in different Facebook groups where you just show up and add value. Then you're the weirdo that shows up and adds value and not saying, "Buy my stuff!" When someone adds value and doesn't ask for anything in return, you better believe every single person that cares about that answer is going to your profile to find out what you're about. It breaks the static because they're not used to it. A person actually helping and taking time out of their own day? And not asking for anything in return? Insanity! Make sure your profile is ready for people to check out.

Sales Pages and Profiles

Always have a link to your free (lead) Facebook groups on your profiles so you can get to the place where you nurture them. The nurturing doesn't happen in public; it happens in this free group. You tease it out in public, then you direct them to your free group where you do the training every week or however often you do it.

The sales all happen in the group. You launch once then make it evergreen. I do that with everything. That means I don't go through a launch, relaunch, relaunch again process, which I don't enjoy. I launch once and it exists. People can sign up for it whenever they want to sign up for it. Do I have other senses of urgency? Of course. But it all happens within the group.

Have testimonials of people who have been through your programs in the group and keep them in the units section. People read reviews. Testimonials are gold nuggets and people don't treat them that way. They are free and the best way to show that someone else just like them is doing this thing and seeing results.

We can talk about what we do in our programs all day long, but it doesn't matter unless they actually see other people getting results.

Omnipresence

You can set yourself up like a movie star to people in the way you show up on your social media. I had a coach message me the other day saying he opened Facebook, and I was literally the first three videos he saw.

That is omnipresence. You need to always be top of mind, because if you are not top of mind, they are not thinking about you. That says nothing about you as a person, but from a marketing and a service perspective, if we are not in front of the people we are here to serve, we cannot serve.

I do it with my videos that go everywhere and posting in my groups once or twice a day. If I go about my day and there is something I think my audience might laugh at or that might lighten their mood, I make a quick post about it. That keeps me top of mind with them.

I'm not talking about the same thing over and over. For example, my husband and I were in the arts district in Dallas, and we saw a painting that looked like our dog Herman with a giant poo next to him. I thought it was so cute, so I took a picture, put it on Facebook, and said, "Hey guys, should we get this picture of Herman with a giant poo next to him?"

There was a ton of activity on it. I wasn't trying to get likes or shares; I was trying to stay top of mind. I was trying to stay relevant, feel the pulse of my audience, and commune with them. I was saying, "We are in this together, and I am not just here to sell you stuff."

When it comes to omnipresence, don't just push things onto those people; bring them in to where you are at so they can all have fun with each other. It's building a community. Sometimes it is just living your life, because your life might seem normal to you, but for the people you serve, you're showing them the transformation they would like to achieve.

Going Global

One of the big shifts that has happened in the last two years is that global interconnectivity has become the new normal. For so many years, people have thought, *I want to start a business.* They thought about a local business; they thought about building a business in their hometown or in their state. But now the entire globe is available. If your audience speak the same language as you, they are potentially your audience.

We're in a unique position to be able to positively impact the world at scale. And every individual—regardless of education level, regardless of anything else—every single individual on the planet has access and ability to be able to do this. So all you have to do is learn how to play the game. And you can play the game at scale.

Whenever I teach how to play the game, I teach how to play the game and have a positive impact at scale. There's also people who want to have a negative impact at scale, but those won't be my people; I would drive them crazy in like two minutes. But people that want to change the world in a positive way—we're going to get along great.

What Are the Skills You'll Need to Go Global?

One primary skill: You need to know how to type or talk.

I think it was Bruce Lee who said that you have to empty your cup to be able to fill it with something else. Essentially, you need to be okay with what you thought was true not being true. So there's some cognitive dissonance that you need to be okay with going through. Because we've been told as people that we aren't able to do this stuff. Your brain believes that, but if you can be open, if you can bypass that cognitive dissonance, you can open yourself up to a global audience. All you have to do is be open to understanding that this doesn't need to be difficult at all. And you just need to be able to turn a computer on and type or talk.

If you're reading this and you're thinking, *I really want to start to make a global impact, to build a global business*, the message isn't "Oh, you need to get good at YouTube. And you need to be a Facebook genius, or whatever social media platform is hot right now." That's not that important. What's really important is that you start to actually question the messages that well-meaning people in your life have given you. It could be messages such as "You can't run a global business from your bedroom."

Now, the tools of technology are so plentiful that all you need to do is just decide to start going down that road, and then give yourself a little bit of grace to learn the tools that are right for your particular audience. Whether that's YouTube, whether that's social media, whether that's presenting in front of a camera or telling great stories in your blog posts. Whatever that is, you're going to develop that. But the important thing is that you become agnostic as to which platform, and you start thinking about being a storyteller, a leader who serves.

A good amount of my clients found me when I was coaching and consulting within a network marketing business. So many people were doing all the "right" things, they were trying really hard to make that system work but not having the success they really wanted.

Deb McCue

CANCER SURVIVOR, ENTREPRENEUR

For the first time in my life, I am more connected with myself. I feel empowered to know myself. And in discovering my uniqueness, I've been able to understand how I can take that and share it with others in a way that might empower them to

Photo courtesy of Debbie McCue

experience the same or consider something that maybe they hadn't before.

Doing this work has affected my life personally but also the lives of my husband and my children as well. We had become very complacent with our children but are now bringing them along on this journey and helping them see that they get to own their lives and their passions.

In my professional life, my confidence has soared. I recently received a promotion where I was able to negotiate an increased salary which freed up my schedule to spend more time with my family. The biggest difference is seeing the possibility of building a business on the side. I've been able to find an alternative to the old way of working. It's really changed my view of the future.

Building the business has been very interesting, it's not about the old way of thinking—products and pricing—but being able to identify a way to fill the needs of others that comes from your heart; that's the secret to the new business model. It's you as a person delivering yourself to others on a totally different level. Knowing that showing up as myself is enough to help others is a completely different mindset.

I was able to identify something in myself that would resonate with others and help others, and that's a totally different kind of business. It's exciting getting up in the morning and doing that kind of work.

Going through Martha's program made me realize that my joy is my life with my family, and the fact that I can take that passion and help others with it will make it never feel like a job. I get to live my joy every day. The power of doing work that is deeply meaningful and totally aligned with the areas that I'm passionate about brings success in every respect. It brings joy in showing up, brings meaning to the work, and has actually developed financial success as well.

The potential is there to not only replace my current salary but replace it multiple times over. It's much larger than just replacing money; it's giving me more free time and doing more meaningful work. When you're at your job, there's a certain personality of the company that you work with, a character and an expectation of methodologies and values that they have. You are fortunate if some of those values coincide with yours or some of the approaches or the personalities; you're lucky if you find that in your day job. Oftentimes you find yourself having to adapt yourself to fit in with this other world. The idea that you can be your true self and thrive and help others thrive is a gift.

It's freedom.

So many people can't imagine themselves being able to have the freedom to be themselves. When I joined the program, there was a fundamental mindset change. I remember the moment it happened. I was in a meeting at work and a coworker told me I always had this weird way I looked at things. I took it very personally. I don't think they were trying to insult me but rather pointing out that

I didn't fit the mold all the time. I did an Aroma Freedom Technique (AFT) session (in HBR) and one of my realizations was that I am unique, and in that uniqueness, I can show up and I can be special. I am worthy. I am able to be unique, and I am worthy of it.

I think that many people will look at this program as a way of doing business from home. I'm trying to flip that viewpoint. There's lots of ways to make money from home just by virtue of connecting with the right company. The true home-based revolution starts within your home, with your own family. If you allow yourself to go through the process of identifying what kind of home you want, it will start a revolution in your home. Having a revolution within yourself and within your home is what's going to propel you forward. It's two very different meanings of the word *home* and the business part that goes with it.

I fell into the supermom/superwoman status. I had this great job, had a decent income, and my husband was willing to stay home with the kids. I was not prepared for what happened next. I found out I had cancer. It was a unique kind of cancer for someone my age. It was a huge point of reflection for me. Was this the life I wanted to pursue? After a certain point, the exit strategy becomes very difficult. My family was depending on me. I had to tell myself that I wasn't going to give up, that I would have the health and endurance to keep going for my family. I started changing things to improve not only my physical health but my mental health as well. It was on this journey that I discovered Martha, and since then, my path has been lighting up in front of me. I'm so grateful for these moments of discovery.

Nowadays, I've put my health as a priority. I was able to surpass running the one hundred miles I pledged for the American Cancer Society fundraiser. I've been able to dedicate each run to either someone who is fighting cancer or someone who lost their fight to cancer. It has brought an awareness to something that is meaningful to me. It's been an experience that has helped my family grow closer together and learn more about each other.

My husband retired from his job of thirty-four years and is starting his own business. I've learned different strategies on how to show up in service on social media. I'm in the process of writing my own book. I never thought it was possible because of my severe dyslexia. My hope is to inspire others to pursue their passions no matter what. I plan on a very whimsical launch of my book, called *I Did It*, and with that will come both one-on-one and group coaching. There will be resources, an online course, and classes that I will offer. Eventually it will turn into podcasts and mastermind weekend sessions that will impact people all over the world to create a revolution inside their own homes. Going through life, there is an abundance of "I did it" moments. There's a freedom to make your own choices and go after your goals. As you get older, some of these decisions are very defining and take you more down a road of permanency. Then you have a family, and your children grow up, and you start to segue from a participant to an observer of these moments. There's an appreciation and an energy that starts to swirl. That's what's critical in this world—that we don't tap out of those moments, that we continue to tap into them as we grow. The world doesn't stop. No one can tell you that you're in your prime for a certain amount of time, because your prime is your whole life.

Tap into your prime and start living!

Since the Beginning of Network Marketing, It's Been Weird

They haven't changed the style of marketing that they've been doing for years. The different network marketing companies were telling their people to use certain strategies in order to grow their businesses, and that has never ever changed since the whole industry began. Many of these businesses started in the forties or fifties. And now we're in 2021—that's almost one hundred years of this system being around and remaining unchanged. The world has changed massively in that amount of time; almost everything is topsy-turvy different than what it was in the forties, fifties, and sixties.

So that style of marketing that they were trying to teach and that was working for them back then wasn't working for me or lots of people. They're saying, *Well, this worked once, so it's gonna always work*, and they just never changed it.

The thing is it doesn't work anymore. What they were doing is a style of push marketing, quite frankly, and push marketing doesn't work very well anymore. Push marketing is when you say, "Hey, buy my stuff, buy my stuff, buy my stuff, buy my stuff." And it's just rapid fire, and eventually, somebody's gonna be like, *Oh, fine, I'll buy their stuff.*

It's kind of pestering people to buy. And sometimes we buy it, because we love it. But so often people will buy it just to get rid of you. Is that the business you want to be creating? Does your ideal customer want to buy something just to get rid of you? Probably not, right?

Continuing to use the old methods because that is what has always been done just wasn't working for me. Well-meaning people that have families and that were putting their eggs in that basket were just not able to find success. They start to think it's them; they start to think there's something wrong with them.

And all the while it's the system. So I come in with a fresh perspective. Because I've never done network marketing before I jumped into this company, I was not gonna sell using the push marketing methods. I was not joining to become a salesperson, because I was snobby. And I thought, I make real businesses. I was like, *That's adorable, but I do real business.* Yeah, I admit it—I was a snob, friends!

Then I started to look into the company I was with. I started looking into what they had. *All right,* I thought. *This could actually be really easy.* So I came in with my fresh perspective of my marketing mind. I could change it into something that feels good to me and something that isn't going to make people avert their eyes as they walk down the hallway or avoid me at a family reunion. You know, where everybody's like, *Don't talk to her; she's totally gonna sell you something.* I could really make something great out of this.

I started doing the stuff that I now teach in HBR on a micro level. I created a system for these network marketers, and it just completely blindsided everyone. Everybody in the industry began to ask, *Why have we not been doing this before?*

I made my own personal strategy of HBR available after the network marketing thing. The network marketing piece is so specific to just that income stream, then I realized, *Oh, you guys want to see how I do everything? Sure, no problem.* That's what HBR is.

Pricing Strategy

I get made fun of for my prices, actually. Some people think it's brilliant, and others think it's dumb. (Keep in mind, the people that think it's dumb are the people overcharging like crazy in my opinion. They think I'm dumb for not charging more. Little do they realize that money isn't my goal, impact is.)

Some people think I need to charge way, way more than I do. But my take on pricing is that I'm not looking to positively impact a low number of people's lives; I'm looking to positively impact a lot of people's lives. And in order to be able to do that, I have to have the price at a place that they're going to be able to afford or else they're not going to be able to be positively impacted. Period. Cue mic drop.

My pricing strategy is very, very simple.

It's all about finding your sweet spot.

And the sweet spot is where you don't feel like you're ripping somebody off, and you don't feel like they're ripping you off.

The low end of it is where you've priced yourself so low that whenever you work with somebody, it almost feels like they're stealing from you. You get frustrated and you feel like you don't want to be there, because you haven't been properly compensated.

The high end of it is that you feel like you're ripping people off, and nobody wants to feel that way.

The sweet spot is right between those two.

And everybody asks, "Well, what's the right price for this program or that product?"

You need to determine what compensation looks like for you. I'll usually walk clients through that conversation. "Okay, well what feels like too low? What feels too high?"

How does it feel?

And then if it feels good, stay with it.

If it doesn't feel good, you need to change it.

It's a very anti-establishment approach to pricing. It's one that really, really works though.

Most people probably underpriced themselves.

And there are some people that I believe are overpricing themselves. Those are usually dudebros with Ferraris and Facebook ads.

Whenever I see someone overpricing themselves, it looks from the outside like they're attempting to price themselves into a luxury niche. And in my world, and in my opinion, they're focused on the wrong thing. Because they're focused on dollars and material gain instead of *Who am I going to serve? And how am I going to change their life?*

There are the conspicuous examples of dudes with Ferraris trying to sell that lifestyle, and I think most people can see that a mile off. But by far, the greatest majority of people we experience are probably underpricing themselves. For so many people, they're probably pricing at their comfort level. But that's a real mistake, because you're thinking about it from your perspective, not from your clients' perspective, or even from the perspective of how much value you add to them.

I recently had someone message me about their pricing. "I'm going to do group coaching," they said. "And I'm going to charge $19 a month."

I was like, *Wait, what???? Um, you're seriously undervaluing yourself right now.*

What people try to do, especially when it comes to group coaching, is to think about it from the wrong perspective.

Here's an example of what I consider to be an unproductive approach. One piece of advice I've seen given is that if you know how much money you want to make at the end, then you need to figure out how many people you want in your group and divide by that, and that's how you come up with your price. Okay, sounds logical but doesn't actually make any sense at all.

Another person has said that you should be charging them by how many hours it took you to create your program or course.

First of all, we need to understand, if it's a course, where it's at in the hierarchy. For example, if you are establishing the fact that you're their guide and building your credibility, price should not be a big speed bump to get over. It should be a very easy, low barrier to entry for them to be able to just take out their wallet and say, *Hey, let me give it a go. Let me just see what this person's about. Let me see if I can work with them.* And then you start moving up from there.

You can't just say, *Well, this took me five hours to make. I charged $250 an hour, so you're going to pay $1,500.*

What we should be doing is talking about what we're selling, what we're offering, how we're serving. And we need to think about what that's going to do in someone's life. What value is that going to bring to somebody? What transformation is going to happen to this person? And what is that worth to them?

If I'm able to turn you into a billionaire, then I can charge whatever I like to turn you into a billionaire.

Value-Based Pricing

In addition to your pricing being in that sweet spot, a fundamental change that people reading this book really need to make is that we need to consider what value it adds to a person's life. It's really easy to understand that if what you do is help people advertise or do marketing, that's simply the value of another client to your business. Then that's really easy to calculate that value. But at a deeper level, what's the value of having your husband not have to work at a job he hates? What's the value of your family? Being able to spend time together as your children are growing up? That's a measurable value that people will be subconsciously calculating when they look at your price.

Or what's the value of learning some health strategies around autoimmune disease or the psychology and negative impact of perfectionism? What is the value of that? How does that impact someone's life? And what's the value of *that*?

For example, consider the cost of getting sick (if what you're teaching people to do is stay healthy). Well, the cost of not being healthy these days is measurable.

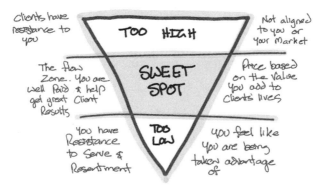

PRICING SWEET SPOT

Clients have resistance to you

TOO HIGH

Not aligned to you or your Market

The flow Zone. You are well paid & help get great Client Results

SWEET SPOT

Price based on the value you add to Clients' lives

You have Resistance to Serve & Resentment

TOO LOW

You feel like you are being taken advantage of

Most People will price their Services based on Comparing themselves to other Competitors. Instead I'd Suggest you switch to a Value-based pricing Model.

What we're not saying is that if it's going to cost you $30,000 to get better that you charge $30,000 for your course. Instead, what you do is to quantify the hidden costs for people so they can calculate the value of your material in their life. Now a $1,200 course that will prevent a $30,000 medical bill looks like a pretty great value.

If you're reading this, you may find yourself doing an inventory around what is that value for all sorts of things. Like this book. Even though you might not be able to initially see the value, think about the example of our HBR members teaching people to overcome some of their mindsets and build a business that works for their lifestyle. Well, the value in that is enormous—not only monetarily but in terms of satisfaction and happiness as well.

This switch from marketplace pricing, or pricing your product based on what you would be prepared to pay, is a very important shift. It really needs to shift to *let's have a look at what the value of that is in someone else's life.* And start to think about pricing from that perspective.

CHAPTER SEVEN

It's Your Revolution

What People Appreciate about HBR

People appreciate the support of other people doing what they are trying to do. Everyone is reaching. They are jumping out the window into this life where they are absolutely going to do well. But if they take the jump by themselves, maybe they will make it and maybe they won't. If you take that jump with thousands of other people, you have a parachute of people with you, all working together and supporting each other in their own endeavors.

Some people like those moms I was talking about earlier team up and start working together. Others bring other people in the group in as experts into their own groups and everyone works with each other. They share their wins. Last night someone shared that they made almost $2,000 last WEEK only a couple of months in. She shared in order to show people it really is possible and happening. Another woman just made $150,000 this month—just five months in!

It's not just business, and it is not even just money. It is people remembering their worth, remembering who they really are, what they desire to do in this life, and doing it. They're doing it together, and they're supported.

I believe these people, when they reach the end of their lives, will feel very satisfied in the way they showed up. They left it all on the court. They used their gifts until the end. This is what I believe we're here for.

Teresa Sanderson has been a registered nurse for more than thirty years. And always yearned to be an entrepreneur. The freedom and the creativity that is lacking in the medical industry for so many was calling, loudly.

Teresa shares a little of what she has learned.

Teresa Sanderson
From Nurse to Video Queen

After just four months in the HBR program, I was able to grow my lead group from zero to two hundred sixty members. I have launched four courses (two of which were written and prepared before I got into HBR) and made money on every product offering I've had.

Photo by Greg Sanderson Photography

Launching a product with sales is new to me because prior to HBR I'd had many failures, even though I'd spent thousands of dollars on training and software. I had launch after launch with no sales, high ad spending, and nothing coming in to cover expenses. Martha's way of teaching and leading is so contra to what is taught in the mainstream business world.

And it works.

I work with forty-something women entrepreneurs who dream of leaving the 9 to 5 to live a life they love. One of the biggest struggles for women entrepreneurs is replacing their income so they can leave their 9 to 5 jobs and feel secure coming home. That is my niche. I empower women entrepreneurs to create income quickly at home through systems that don't take all of their time but generate income to fuel their dreams.

I have five established income streams including online courses, affiliate marketing, network marketing, video marketing and voice-over services, and business coaching. I have plans to launch a course for nurses to help them become continuing education providers and to write my first book by September this year. Being part of this program has been very exciting and has prepared me for the success I can clearly see ahead.

All of this has empowered me to make a meaningful income even as I was just getting started. I started making money on my courses and video marketing services within two weeks. Being able to contribute to the household budget has been so positive for me.

Connecting with my audience, though—that has been an entirely different thing! And an unexpected joy.

The messages that I receive from the people I help are such a blessing to me. And when one of my video students in the initial launch of the course got paid for a video she created before the course was even finished, I was elated! That one thing validated that I was able to help other women duplicate what I had done with video marketing and voice-over. What a great feeling!

Life is so different for me now. Rather than just dragging myself to work, I enjoy life now. I spend Friday afternoons with my grandchildren. I take walks with my dogs several times each day. Life is good.

I left my nursing job abruptly five months ago due to a flare-up of depression. This was brought on by the stress of my work, and to add to that, my husband and I now had the stress of having 60 percent less income. As I began to explore options for my own future, I found HBR. It was through the first two weeks of mindset work in the program that I nurtured myself like no other time in my life.

As someone with depression, I am no stranger to talk therapy and have done it for years. But the mental work I was doing in HBR was so powerful, and I have been able to release so many negative memories and false beliefs. This has been so life-giving for me, and has taken the brakes off my hopes and dreams.

I now see my own value clearly, and I teach my world how to value me. All from a business course?!?

What I never expected was the mindset work in HBR that would be so life-giving to me. I had been through several years of talk therapy before entering HBR and had not released my failures and past negative experiences. In HBR, I was able to release the weight of my past failures and truly know my own worth. The work in conscious language and Aroma Freedom Technique (AFT) has helped me prepare for my success and step into it fully. I jumped into HBR to learn how to grow a business. The blessings I've gained in being able to know my own value and love and accept myself were totally unexpected but sorely needed in my life.

My life has changed from working in the stressful field of nursing to now working at home on our rural homestead. My self-care is easy. Life is balanced and joyful. Even when I have a down day from depression, I am in charge of my schedule and can be flexible to care for myself. That's made such a huge difference to my happiness.

There are three things I learned that have made this possible.

How to grow a business without a high dollar ad spend, or even no ad spend at all.

How to sell high ticket items and understand the real value of my experience.

And most important, that the world needs my voice and my message.

One of the greatest discoveries has been that it is possible to grow an online business without spending money on ads. I really expected that I needed to find a lot of money for advertising, but that's just not true.

When I think of an entrepreneur, I think of someone who is super busy, wearing all of the hats, doing all of the things to keep the business going.

That image of an exhausted, frazzled business owner always struggling to make ends meet. In the last four months I've come to see an entrepreneur as someone who is relaxed, enjoys life, enjoys the work she does, and has time for the important things in life.

Here is what I want all the readers of this book to know:

Live your life with intention. Dream big, and make a plan.

Acknowledgments

To my husband, Mike, who has always held the string to my balloon.

And to my daughter, Norah, to whom I can attribute this whole crazy ride.

These two people mean everything to me; they are my inspiration, they are my anchors, and they are Mommy's biggest fans. I love you two so much!

I would also like to thank my students and fans. Thank you for believing in me and pushing me to always reach further and further out to make sure this message makes it to the far reaches of this world. You make me so proud every day as you continue to show up in your own worlds and change the status quo to be more accommodating to families doing things in a different way.

Now let's GO!!

XO,
Martha

Additional Resources

If reading this book has sparked an interest to explore how you can create your own home-based revolution, here are some resources.

The Home-Based Revolution

Heart-Centered + Succesful (my own group where I share tons of tutorials and trainings and also has the 90 Days Side Gig to Main Gig Challenge): www.marthaekrejci.com/wahm

Martha's Facebook page:
www.facebook.com/martha.krejci1111

Martha's YouTube channel:
watchmartha.com

And grab some free goodies and resources that will constantly be updated, so be sure to check back often at withmartha.com/hbrbookresources.

Books I've Loved

The Secret by Rhonda Byrne: Author Rhonda Byrne, like each of us, has been on her own journey of discovery. In *The Secret*, she explains with simplicity the law that is governing all lives and offers the knowledge of how to create—intentionally and effortlessly—a joyful life.

Now for the first time in history, all the pieces of *The Secret* come together in a revelation that is life transforming for all who experience it.

Link: https://amzn.to/3qYvOX0
Hint: this ^ is what an affiliate link looks like :)

The rest of my preferred book list is at
withmartha.com/hbrbookresources

Finally, in closing, I would LOVE for you to stay in touch with me on social media so I can watch you grow. It truly FEEDS my SOUL.

About the Author

Martha is a self-proclaimed high-vibin' mama, wife, and lover of life first, and business growth strategist and investor second.

She made her first million in less than a year using a strategy she teaches openly, no fluff, no lies, no half-truths. She teaches it all in HBR that is by invite only; message her for details.

She's a social media marketing powerhouse that has taken the interwebs by storm.

Martha has been featured in *O, The Oprah Magazine*, *Fast Company*, *Cosmopolitan*, *Shape*, and HuffPost, among other places, for her innate, intuitive marketing expertise.

Today, she is showing everyday people how to build a business that is heart-centered, service focused, and never ever leaves people feeling salesy or sold to.

Come and fill your cup—and it will probably be legit overflowing—but it's all good; you will leave ready to take on the world!